Unforgiven

Unforgiven

Liz McGregor

Jonathan Ball Publishers
Johannesburg · Cape Town · London

All rights reserved.
No part of this publication may be reproduced or transmitted,
in any form or by any means, without prior permission
from the publisher or copyright holder.

© Text Liz McGregor 2022
© Published edition 2022 Jonathan Ball Publishers

Originally published in South Africa in 2022 by
JONATHAN BALL PUBLISHERS
A division of Media24 (Pty) Ltd
PO Box 33977
Jeppestown
2043

ISBN 978-1-77619-188-8
eBook ISBN 978-1-77619-189-5

Every effort has been made to trace the copyright holders and to obtain their permission for the use of copyright material. The publishers apologise for any errors or omissions and would be grateful to be notified of any corrections that should be incorporated in future editions of this book.

Website: www.jonathanball.co.za
Twitter: www.twitter.com/JonathanBallPub
Facebook: www.facebook.com/JonathanBallPublishers

Cover by Wilna Combrinck
Design and typesetting by Catherine Coetzer
Set in Sabon
Printed and bound by CTP Printers, Cape Town

For Guy, Cathy, Andrew and Simon

Contents

Prologue		9
1	The murder	13
2	The trial	24
3	In the cane fields	45
4	The verdict	54
5	Bastard fate strikes again	59
6	Weaving it all together	73
7	Alexander and Nongoloza	83
8	Wouldn't hurt a fly	104
9	When the earth shook	116
10	'The batons slip out of your hands when they are covered in blood'	134

11	Can Liz stop?	157
12	'I have traded my shackles for a glorious song'	161
13	Quartalehouse in the Cape	174
14	Meeting at Martins	191
15	Martins, Take 2	201
16	Martins, Take 3	213
17	Preparation	221
18	Voorberg	227
19	The meeting	234
20	What I've learnt	245
Epilogue		253
Acknowledgements		259
Glossary		261
References		263

Prologue

Two days after we bury my mother's ashes, my father is murdered.

On 9 August 2008, the first anniversary of her death, he drives in from his home in Tulbagh, about a hundred and twenty kilometres northeast of Cape Town, and picks me up from a friend's flat in Green Point. I have been the keeper of the casket containing her ashes. Yesterday, I flew down from Johannesburg with it on my lap.

Dad stands on my doorstep, pale and near to tears. He barely slept the night before, he says. As I pick the casket up from the table, he averts his eyes.

Outside he shows me a small dent in the rear bumper of his beloved Mercedes. He reversed into a tree, he says. 'And they want R11 000 to fix it!' But because he is over seventy, he won't have to pay the excess. This small triumph seems to cheer him up.

We drive to Christ Church in Constantia where my siblings, their spouses and children are waiting with the priest under a big oak tree. This, my mother's final resting place, is a compromise. We, her offspring, envisioned a wild, beautiful place where we could scatter her ashes. But every time we tried to talk to my father about it, the tears flowed. He finally agreed to this, an Anglican church on a busy road.

My elder brother Guy and my sister Cathy say a few words about my mom. Sabine, my niece, plays the flute. Dad just stands there, weeping. When the priest tries to bless the casket, Dad wrests it from him and drops the ashes, still in their plastic bag, into a hole that has been dug under the tree.

Afterwards, we have lunch at Groot Constantia wine estate: two tables – one for the ten children and one for the ten adults. All immediate family. 'Look what you've spawned, Dad. Aren't you proud?' I say to him. He nods, still teary. As we slide into a slow, gentle afternoon, he begins to rally.

He realises that he needs to find a companion, he says. He can keep busy till 5 p.m. but then he gets very lonely. He tells us with some amusement that he mentioned this to someone in the village and on the last couple of evenings he noticed a woman walking slowly down the road below his house. It seemed she wanted to get a good look at him before declaring her availability.

At 3 p.m., we all go down to the pub next door to watch the Springboks play Argentina. At 4 p.m., when

Prologue

it is clear our lads are winning, he says he is ready to go back home.

It is to be the last time I see him. Some time between 10 p.m. and midnight on 11 August, he is murdered.

Robin McGregor

I

The murder

At 8 a.m. on 12 August, my cellphone rings. I am still in the Green Point flat, making coffee. It is my brother, Guy. A bit early in the morning for a social call, I think. But I answer brightly enough.

His response is terse. 'Liz, the police called. They found Dad's car in Bellville last night.' A pause. And then, in a rush: 'Liz, he's been murdered.'

My first thought is that this is some sort of macabre joke. But at the same time, I feel myself beginning to hyperventilate.

Liza, my sister-in-law, comes on the line. 'Liz, he isn't joking. It's true.'

The shock is what I remember most vividly: panicky, breathless, wailing out loud like a mad woman. Part of me still thinks it can't possibly be true. I have to get out there and see for myself. He will be in his house

– injured, maybe, but alive and able to explain all this himself. I run out to my car and drive down Strand Street to the N1 – the northbound highway that heads straight through the interior, to Johannesburg and up to Zimbabwe – wailing, barely able to see through my tears. I take a wrong turn and find myself, an hour later, in Ceres. Frantic now, convinced I will be driving around for the rest of the day unless I get help, I stop at the police station.

'My father's been murdered in Tulbagh,' I sob to a startled policeman, 'and I don't know how to get there!'

'Wait,' he says. And within minutes a police car draws up next to mine and leads me to the turnoff to Tulbagh.

Cathy, my youngest brother Simon and their spouses are already there, standing around in the road. There is a police cordon around the house and several police cars outside.

'Dad's in the house,' says my brother. 'They won't let us in.'

A blond man, a detective inspector, introduces himself. They have two men in custody, he says. A forensics team is searching the house for clues.

Guy and Liza arrive. We all stand around outside in the hot sun, barely able to speak, even to each other. A mortuary van draws up and the driver disappears inside the house. Shortly afterwards, a stretcher with an oblong shape enclosed in a white plastic bag is wheeled out. My dad. The van drives off with him in it.

We drift down to Paddagang, a restaurant a couple of

The murder

streets away, and set up camp on their terrace. It's a tranquil place, with its vine-covered trellises and yellow weaver birds popping in and out; my dad was a frequent customer. They are good to us, bringing us tea and platters of sandwiches and pastries and not letting us pay.

During those dazed hours, we slowly face up to practicalities. His grandchildren, sister and close friends have to be told before they hear it on the news. Bank cards have to be cancelled.

The media have started calling. Dad was catapulted to fame in the eighties when his research revealed how a handful of companies monopolised South Africa's wealth. He became a crusader against the excessive power of big firms, motivated largely by how this power punished the poor.

The police phone and ask for one of us to go to the morgue to identify the body. Guy volunteers. He returns a couple of hours later. Dad had raised his arm to protect his face, he says. It had frozen in that position. It was the first clue to how brutal the murder had been.

All the time, I am desperate to get into the house. This won't feel real till I see his house without him in it.

The last time I was in it was a few weeks ago. Dad had asked me and Cathy to help him decide where to hang his pictures. The renovations he'd embarked on after buying the house a few months previously were almost complete and he proudly showed off the results. He'd knocked down internal walls to create three large rooms: a living and dining area, an office, and his bedroom.

He'd contracted the builder who built the house – who was from the nearby town of Saron – to do the renovations. Each room contained a large flat-screen TV. In his office, a carpenter was building him an L-shaped desk. An alcove between the lounge and the bedroom had been fitted with floor-to-ceiling shelves to house his precious collection of Africana books.

A favourite aunt of his had died recently, and with the money she'd left him he'd had his garden landscaped: half-grown olive trees, interspersed with lavender bushes, lined the borders. In the centre was a wild fig, his and my mother's favourite tree. Two fledgling walnut trees flanked the veranda. He was planning to put a sign up saying 'Zoe's Garden' in honour of his aunt.

The house was anything but peaceful that day. We brought lunch – his favourite, lamb sausages and mashed potato, followed by fresh mango. Workmen wandered in and out and we ate to the accompaniment of hammering and drilling.

He showed us a new safe he had bolted to the back wall of his bedroom cupboard. Alongside it was a second safe, identical. He said he wanted a separate safe to house his two revolvers. The old one contained cash. He was fretting about the new safe because he had somehow managed to lock it without setting the new combination.

That evening, he phoned to say he had managed to open the safe.

It isn't until the following afternoon, two days after the murder, that we are finally allowed into the house.

The murder

The detective comes out into the street where my sister and I are waiting and accompanies us inside. On the veranda another policeman waits, a small, dark-skinned man. He stands up and puts out his hand: 'Detective Inspector Bailey. I am in charge of the investigation into your father's murder.'

It's bad, he warns. Are you sure you want to see it? I say yes. I need to see everything. I need to understand exactly what happened.

The French windows leading from the veranda into the house are smashed. The police had to break in because the killer locked the house and took the keys with him when he drove off in my dad's car.

The first thing I see are his glasses. They are on the kitchen counter and the lenses are coated in blood. A miniature grandfather clock he inherited from his father lies on the floor, its walnut frame still intact, splinters of glass scattered around it like a halo. Beside it lies a photograph of him and my mother on their wedding day – my mother smiling broadly in her white veil, my father looking happy, if a little dazed. I remember holding it against the wall, shifting it up and down while he and my sister deliberated on the best position.

Individual portraits of each of their five offspring, frozen in childhood, line the walls, undisturbed. Guy, Cathy, Andrew, Simon and me: all born within six years to my devoutly Catholic mother who, to my agnostic father's dismay, refused to use contraception.

Blood streaks map out his last journey as he was

dragged up the passage, and pool outside his bedroom door where he was left while his murderer hammered off the two safes hidden in his bedroom cupboard, leaving bloody footprints stamped into the white carpet.

His bed is neatly made, one corner turned down in a triangle.

The detectives explain, haltingly, gently, that they assume the killer surprised Dad in the hallway and then dragged his body into the bathroom where the windows are high up and opaque. This was so that no one looking through the windows would see him. The footprints are useless for identification because the killer kept his socks on. There are no fingerprints because he wore gloves.

One of the detectives asks me to look around to see what has been taken. The TVs and two computers are still there: all that appears to be missing are those two safes in the bedroom. And his car.

Someone has to go to the offices of the Bellville South Organised Crime Unit to formally identify the car. I volunteer, still haunted by a sense of unreality, driven by an obsessive need to see evidence of my dad's death.

It is a newish-looking face-brick building alongside the Bellville South police station. DI Bailey is summoned and he leads me to a yard full of cars. There is Dad's, covered in a fine, dark powder. For fingerprints, says Bailey. It will wash off.

The murder

I didn't know his registration number but it is the right model and colour – and, most tellingly, there is a familiar dent in the boot.

He reveals that they found a tik lolly inside, a glass pipe used to smoke tik – the street name for crystal methamphetamine. There were also palm prints, which had been traced to a local prostitute.

I turn away, sickened by the sordidness of it. My dad loved that car and took pride in keeping it immaculate.

—

The weeks following the murder are a blur. I remember frequent, embarrassing outbursts of hysterical sobbing; drinking too much to relax enough to get to sleep and jerking awake a couple of hours later, rigid with anxiety. I lose all sense of personal safety, convinced that around every corner lurks an assailant, knife poised.

At Christmas, our broken family gathers in the south coast seaside village of Arniston, about two hundred kilometres from Cape Town, as usual. Without our parents to hold us together, we are fractured, each marooned in separate islands of grief and guilt. One of my brothers confides that he blames himself because he didn't do enough to ensure my father was safe. I find this heartbreaking. No one could have told my father what to do. He always danced to his own tune.

I end up spending New Year's Eve in hospital in Somerset West, after a two-and-a-half-hour operation to rebuild a shattered knuckle on my right hand using bone taken from my elbow. I did something stupid and reckless: swam at the harbour at high tide and then tried to get out at a particularly rocky spot instead of the slipway I usually used. I had gripped a rock, my fingers finding handy holes, when a huge wave hit me from behind and knocked me head over heels, snapping the knuckle. I remember weeping bitterly as I burdened the anaesthetist with the details of my father's murder.

I realise I have to get help, and consult a psychotherapist recommended by a friend. But she insists that, before we can deal with the trauma of the murder, we have to explore my relationship with my father, starting at birth. I sit in her tasteful consulting rooms, gazing out at Table Mountain, and think, I can't do this.

Instead, I go to my GP, who loads me up with drugs: to sleep, to calm me down, to stem the leaking grief. It works. Within weeks, I start sleeping through the night and slowly begin to regain a sense of equilibrium. I also gain 10 kilograms, which is less welcome but a price worth paying. Or so it seems at the time.

What also saves me, less expectedly, is rugby.

When the Springboks won the Rugby World Cup in France in 2007, my publisher had a brainwave: a book by a woman on rugby might be sufficiently counterintuitive to garner a respectable audience. Particularly a woman as ignorant about rugby as I was. This was entirely new territory for me, and it felt like a challenge. I grew up with rugby – my father and three brothers were mad about it and had all played with varying degrees of proficiency. My view of it was that it was nasty and brutish. But politically it was interesting, occupying as it did a visceral position in the psyche of the average white South African male whose status had changed so vastly in the democratic era. My father was delighted to be in a position to educate me on a subject about which I was woefully ignorant.

As the drugs begin to work, I throw myself back into research with renewed enthusiasm. I choose three teams – the Bulls, Western Province and the University of Cape Town's Ikey Tigers – and shadow them through campaigns, finding release in their single-minded absorption. Nothing matters to them except the next game. And, once that is over, their gaze shifts immediately to the following Saturday. Win or lose, the emotions are extreme and overwhelming. I see grown men cry after a loss and it seems nothing can beat the high of a win. Allowing myself to become caught up in this weekly drama takes my own focus away from my deep apprehension about the next hurdle to be crossed.

One of the difficulties of losing a loved one to murder is that closure is so much more complex. With a natural death, you have some control over the grieving process: it is an intimate affair. You can come to terms with the loss at your own pace.

With a murder, there is another actor involved, over whom you have no control. Worse still, there is a bureaucracy – clumsy, slow-moving, with a logic of its own. We had been told that, although the accused had been in custody since the murder, he was pleading not guilty, so the trial had to be put off until sufficient evidence had been gathered. It has been set for April 2010. The date looms over me, another ordeal to be endured.

In the preceding months, I follow the University of Cape Town (UCT) first team's campaign to win the Varsity Cup. One of their key early games is against Nelson Mandela University (NMU). Port Elizabeth, on the Eastern Cape coast and home to NMU, is notoriously windy; the direction and strength of the wind on match day is a major concern and focus of pre-match preparations.

The day before the big game, I am sitting alone in the near-empty stands when I happen to glance at my phone and read the news that the trial is to be postponed. No judges are available in April so it will only start six months later, on 11 October.

Despair floods me with such intensity I can scarcely breathe. Lifting my eyes from my phone, I find my gaze caught by the solitary figure of the fly half, practising kicking at post. I watch as he goes deep inside himself to that still point of pure concentration, apparently oblivious to the howling of the wind and the cries of his teammates passing the ball back and forth at the far end of the field. I follow his swift glance up at the goalposts and back down to the ball as he swings his leg back in one controlled muscular movement and then forward

The murder

until it collides with the ball. I watch him repeat the process over and over until the despair drains away and I feel calm again.

2

The trial

A murder trial is not about the victim. He or she is simply the backdrop to a contest between state and accused, each trying to assert the supremacy of its own narrative.

Judge Nathan Erasmus, in his wig and long, black robe, flanked by two assessors, sits up high on his dais, dominating this courtroom at the Western Cape High Court, which, oak-panelled and high-ceilinged, feels like a theatre in which a drama is to be played out, its denouement yet to be written.

Facing the judge in the front row sits the prosecutor, Advocate Tshoele. To her left is the counsel for the defence, funded by legal aid. Grey-haired, heavy-bellied, he is the only white man among the principals.

The family, like the corpse, is incidental to the central drama.

The trial

Advocate Tshoele has asked me to open the trial with a brief statement about my father. I try to describe what my father meant to me, his daughter, and the political impact of his work. I want the murderer to know the quality of the life he has snuffed out. In the end, though, I am hurried and halting, intimidated and overwhelmed by the presence of the man who has precipitated all this. After saying my piece I slide onto the wooden bench alongside my siblings, among the spectators.

Cecil Thomas, 33, of Saron, is charged with murder, robbery with aggravating circumstances and possession of a firearm. He pleads not guilty to all charges and, as there is little direct evidence linking him to the murder, the case against him has had to be painstakingly assembled.

For the first few days, I cannot bear to look at him. But when I do, I think he seems pathetic: a hunched, harassed-looking man. His nickname is Patat. It means 'sweet potato', and I know from Robert Shell's book *Children of Bondage* that it was a derogatory name given to slaves: this goes through my mind as the chains on his wrists and ankles rattle and clink.

The first person to give evidence after me is the last person, aside from his murderer, to see my father alive. Mike Hunter, owner of the Tulbagh B&B where my father stayed while the renovations on his house were being completed, testifies that, at about 5.30 p.m. on 11 August 2008, he visited my father to see how he had transformed the house. It is a long, narrow property, stretching between two streets: Kriegler Street and Buitenkant Street. After the tour, the two men sat on the veranda that flanked the house on the Buitenkant Street side, with its view of the Saronsberg mountains. Dad had the outside of the house painted a sunflower yellow. A little garish, I thought when I saw it, but he said he found it cheerful. And cheer was what he badly needed.

While my father and Mike were enjoying a whisky on the veranda, a neighbour, Nelia Retief, her partner and her children were taking their dogs for a walk. With her long, blonde-streaked hair and tight jeans tucked into knee-high boots, Nelia cuts a glamorous figure in the witness box. She tells the court that she is an estate agent, and that she had sold the house to my father earlier that year. She lived opposite him, on the Kriegler Street side.

When Nelia and her family returned from their walk, they found a strange man in their driveway. He said he was looking for '*die argitek in die geel huis*' (the architect in the yellow house). Nelia pointed out the '*geel huis*' over the road and said it belonged to a Mr McGregor, who was a publisher, not an architect. The man was wearing gardening gloves, which she thought odd, given that it was not a cold evening.

'Do you see that man here?' asks the judge.

With a flourish, her entire arm extended, Nelia points at Cecil Thomas. 'That is the man!'

Nelia's evidence is crucial to placing Thomas at the scene. It strikes me that she is a brave woman. I know

The trial

that her relationship has since broken down and that she and her children are now living alone in the house opposite where the murder took place.

In an attempt to establish the timeline, the prosecution introduces cellphone records which reveal that, after Mike left, my father had a couple of long conversations – one with my brother Andrew, and one with an old friend from McGregor, a woman, with whom he had recently renewed contact, apparently with a view to a possible romance. She wrote to us afterwards to say they had arranged to meet for lunch.

He then prepared for bed with a long, hot bath, during which he would usually read a novel, his favourite way of winding down for the night.

Next to give evidence is a constable from the Bellville South police station. He says that while he and a colleague were out on a routine patrol, they noticed something out of place: a Mercedes-Benz, its headlights blazing, parked in a driveway. It is a poor area, says the constable, and an expensive car usually points to a drug dealer.

They stopped and got out of the van. Two men standing next to the car tried to run away. When they claimed that the car had nothing to do with them and they had no idea to whom it belonged, they were arrested.

The men were put in the back of the police van and the constable drove them to the Bellville South police station. His colleague followed in the Mercedes.

One of the men was Cecil Thomas. The other, Maurice Bennett, lived in a room behind the house where the car had been parked.

When questioned, Cecil Thomas changed his story. The car, he said, had been given to him by a man he knew as 'Eyes' with the instruction to find a buyer for it. Eyes, he said, was dark-skinned and walked with a limp. He could be found in Voortrekker Road, Bellville South, in a flat above a café called Mr Burger.

This immediately raised an alert. Mr Burger was well known to the police. It was owned by Chris 'Langkop' Arendse, a leader of The Firm, one of Cape Town's most powerful crime syndicates. Arendse was known to specialise in robberies of businesses and houses.

A raid was organised and a man matching the description given to them by Thomas was identified and arrested. The police noted that the man had blood on his jeans and on his white takkies. Eyes' real name was revealed to be Llewellyn Tobias.

I sit there on that hard wooden bench, reeling. This is the first I have heard of gang involvement in the murder. And not just any gang. The Firm was formed in the nineties when gang godfather Colin Stanfield brought gang bosses together and negotiated a 'Pax Mafiosa' – a common front against Pagad, the vigilante group then waging war on the gangs.

The Firm also formed a drugs cartel against another threat. In 1994, South Africa's borders opened to the world and, along with legitimate traders, international criminal syndicates moved in, offering a smorgasbord of exotic new drugs such as heroin and cocaine. Working together, The Firm fought off the foreign threat, negotiating with the foreigners for supply of the new drugs but maintaining their monopoly on distribution and sales.

My attention snaps back to the present. The officer is telling the court that a search of the Mercedes revealed a tik lolly, traces of blood and a wallet containing my father's driver's licence and business cards. When there was no response to the cellphone or landline numbers given on the cards, the police traced the latter to my father's Tulbagh address. The police station there was contacted and an officer sent around to my father's house.

The officer from Tulbagh is called to the stand. He describes how, when he got to my father's house, he was surprised to find the lights were on. This was unusual, he says, given that it was early morning, and he knew from his rounds that my father was not an early riser. I am touched by this, that this young man – he must be in his early twenties and is clearly a bit overwhelmed by the experience of giving evidence in the High Court – cared enough to take note of my father's daily rituals. He explains that when his knocks went unanswered, he peered through the windows and saw pools of blood. A neighbour provided Guy's phone number. The constable called him and got permission to smash the door in. When he discovered the body, he cordoned off the house.

Because my father was a public figure, his-murder was elevated to the Hawks, the specialised crime fighting unit based at the Bellville South Organised Crime Unit at the time. DI Bailey was the officer on duty and he took charge of the investigation. There was extensive media coverage and the pressure on the police to produce a result was intense.

The evidence produced up to now has been fairly straightforward. That now changes, and it becomes complicated and contradictory. It is increasingly clear that at no point was Thomas willing or able to give a truthful – or even credible – account of what transpired that night. Instead, he slipped and slithered through a bewildering series of versions.

The court is told that, confronted with the news that the car found in his possession was linked to a murder, Cecil Thomas again changed his story. At 2.10 p.m. on 12 August, the day after the murder, he signed a new statement in which he said that on the day of the murder, he had met a man near his home who had invited him to go for a beer in the '*schema*' (scheme), a poor area at the back end of Saron. The man asked him how well he knew Tulbagh because he wanted to visit his *tjommie*, his mate – the *argitek* in the *geel huis* – but he didn't know where the house was.

The man revealed that he was in Saron with two friends who had a car, and suggested Thomas go with them to Tulbagh. One of the men was Eyes. The other two men were strangers, and he never learnt their names.

The trial

Once in Tulbagh, the other three men waited at a bar and sent Thomas to look for the yellow house. Once he had located it, the men bought beer and drove up to a viewing point just outside the town, where they drank it. When it began to get dark, they got back into the car, drove down into the town and parked in Buitenkant Street, outside the yellow house.

They then disclosed that they knew the *argitek* had money in the house, and that they were going to '*gou 'n nommer dala*' ('do a quick number'). This, Thomas said, was a reference to a prison gang ritual. Thomas claimed that he had refused to go into the house and was left in the car with the driver, who had a gun. The other two men got out of the car, climbed over the fence and walked towards the house.

The men returned twice with black rubbish bags, which they put in the boot of the car. He noticed, he said, that their hands were red with blood. The third time, only one man returned. Eyes did not. The driver started the car and they drove around to the back of the house, where the garage door and gate stood open. He and the two men drove straight to Bellville, where they stopped outside Mr Burger. Eyes drew up in a bronze Mercedes and told Thomas he had to go and sell it. When Thomas refused, Eyes threatened to kill him. 'I am afraid of Eyes and his friends because they are gangsters and would kill me if they got a chance.'

He then drove the car to the home of his friend, Maurice Bennett, where he was arrested.

I am a journalist. I have covered murder trials in this very court. I have interviewed victims of violence and have done my best to enter imaginatively into their experience to properly convey their pain. But none of it prepared me for the horror of sitting in this stuffy courtroom, day after day, while details of the brutality inflicted on someone with whom I was so intimately connected are revealed in tortuous detail. I am already acquainted with the bare facts around the murder, but the extent of the brutality involved and the sordidness and viciousness of the world that entered mine through the mutilated body of my father comes as a complete shock.

Members of Thomas's family are in court most days and in large numbers. They occupy a couple of rows at the back: mostly soft-faced, rounded women of various generations. During a lunch break, one of them approaches me, wanting to offer condolences, but I shun her – not through anger but more a kind of shutting off, of self-protection. I can't deal with the emotional complexity of separating their pain from the revulsion and fear I feel for the man in the dock.

The daily bombardment of horror is more than I can bear. Although I am still taking handfuls of drugs, it seems my brain has jerked back into that hyperalert state it was in after the murder. Again, I lose my sense of safety: every man in a hoodie seems poised to slice my throat.

I double up the security on my flat on the Atlantic Seaboard, where I live alone. I hardly leave it, aside from the daily trips to court. Danger lurks everywhere. I am plagued by headaches, insomnia and a burning gut.

The days in court are agony, bearable only because I know that at some point they will come to an end. Much of the proceedings are conducted in Afrikaans, so I have to force myself to concentrate.

The state does a good job of demolishing Thomas's story. A Saron man testifies that he found Thomas hitchhiking at the Saron turnoff and gave him a lift into Tulbagh on the afternoon in question. So, the story of being picked up by strange men was clearly nonsense. More decisive evidence comes from my father's keen-eyed neighbour, Jeannette Jansen, and her hyperactive Boerboel. There was no car parked on Buitenkant Street that evening, she says. Firstly, they would have seen it and, secondly, the Boerboel would have 'gone *tekere*' (gone crazy).

Every time the Boerboel barked, reveals Jeannette, she climbed onto the dressing table in her bedroom, from where she could see into my father's house. At 11.50 p.m., she heard the garage door opening and from the vantage point of her dressing table, saw the Mercedes-Benz being driven out into Kriegler Street. She saw the driver wait until the automated gate had shut behind him, before pulling off.

She knew that my brother and his family had spent the day with my father, so she assumed they had a problem of some sort – car trouble, maybe – and that he was going to help them.

The SIM card from my father's phone provided more evidence. Thomas had tried to destroy it to obliterate evidence of who owned it, but experts managed to repair it sufficiently to read its history. Two calls were made to a number in Saron while the murder was in progress. Both went unanswered but were later traced to a childhood friend of Thomas's. Cellphone towers between Tulbagh and Saron revealed that the phone had travelled to Saron at about midnight.

To my surprise, DI Bailey appears in the witness stand. In the weeks leading up to the trial, I tried to get hold of him. He was our point of contact in the police and I hoped to get information from him about what to expect during the trial. But suddenly his cellphone number no longer worked. When I rang the station switchboard, I was told he was no longer with the police, but no one could tell me why. It was perplexing; he had driven the investigation from the start. It also meant we were entirely unprepared for what unfolded in the courtroom.

In the witness stand now, DI Bailey testifies that, during a search of an outbuilding at Thomas's mother's home in Saron, he found one of the safes in an unused deep freeze. Soon afterwards, a local man fishing in the Saron dam hooked a surprising find: a .38 Special Taurus revolver. A search of the police register revealed that the licence was in my father's name.

By the time the morning's session ends, DI Bailey has disappeared. The more I hear in court, the more questions

The trial

I have, which I had hoped he could have helped with. For instance, if the police knew that a notorious gang leader was selling drugs on Voortrekker Road, a major artery and retail centre only a few kilometres away from the Hawks headquarters, why did they not shut it down?

For the next day or two I stay away from court, finding it all too much. But then I force myself to go back. If my father had to endure all of this, the least I can do is bear witness to it.

One bright spring morning a few weeks into the trial, Llewellyn Tobias arrives to give evidence and Cape Town's subterranean world, in the background up to now, floats to the surface in the elegant courtroom. A short, scrawny man, dressed head to toe in black, with a shock of black hair and a diamond stud in one ear, he bristles with a furious energy.

Tobias was originally charged with Thomas but the charges were dropped when he turned state witness. The judge warns him that he could still be charged for possession of stolen goods. He will decide whether to indemnify him once Tobias has given his testimony and the judge believes he had told the truth. The stolen goods charge was in relation to my father's camera.

Speaking in Afrikaans, Tobias identifies himself as a soldier in the 28s.

In prison, he explains, he is known as Eyes because of his peculiarly light-coloured irises. This is the name he prefers to be known by. This blurring of his prison and street identities makes sense in light of what I know about the 28s: they are the dominant wing of the Number gangs, born in the mine compounds and prisons at the turn of the 20th century. Since 1994, they have spread to the streets and are second in size and dominance only to the Americans. Their leader is Ralph Stanfield, nephew and heir to founder of The Firm, Colin Stanfield, who died of cancer in 2004.

Tobias holds up his hand to show the evidence of his street gang affiliation: the letters 'TJ' are tattooed into the skin. This, he explains, stands for the Terrible Josters. In 2019, leaders of the Terrible Josters went on trial on 200 counts: of murder, attempted murder, dealing tik and Mandrax to schoolchildren as well as adults, intimidation, bribery and contravention of the Prevention of Organised Crime Act. The Terrible Josters, who fall under the umbrella of the 28s, is one of the most vicious and powerful gangs currently terrorising the Western Cape. The state asserts that it has 10 000 members.

Yet Tobias evinces outrage at finding himself in court. Shooting furious glances at Thomas from the witness stand, he claims that he barely knows him. The night of the murder was the first time he met Thomas. 'I had only been out of prison for four days and he is trying to frame me for a murder. That is why I am so angry.' He also denies any knowledge of either Tulbagh or Saron, claiming he has only visited the latter once.

Asked for his address, Tobias says he 'sleeps in doorways' – but at the time of the murder he was living

The trial

in a flat above Mr Burger. Ernest Arendse, son of Chris 'Langkop' Arendse, owned the flat. He sold drugs from the flat, which operated as a tik house where customers could smoke the drugs he sold to them. On the day of the murder, he and some friends were at the flat all day and into the evening, drinking on the balcony.

One of the four surveillance cameras trained on the Voortrekker Road entrance to Mr Burger picked up a bronze Mercedes pulling up outside. The driver did not get out, so Eyes went down to investigate. 'A guy comes with a *mooi* [nice] car. This is my chance to make money. The driver was stuttering, and he asked me for a tik lolly.' Tobias points at Cecil Thomas: 'He is the one.'

Then, 'We smoked some tik in the car. Then I saw he didn't know how to handle the car. He couldn't operate the window and I could see he didn't match the car. He said it was his brother's car. He wanted to buy a half gram of tik. He pulled a camera out from between his legs and said he wanted to sell it.'

When the trial ends for the day and my sister, my brother Andrew and I are leaving the court, Andrew decides to pop into the loo. He will meet us at the car, he says.

When we get outside, I see Tobias waiting on the pavement, near to where my car is parked. I say to my sister, 'I don't want Tobias to be able to identify the car as mine. Hopefully, he will have moved on by the time Andrew gets here.' So we walk further up the street and wait in a doorway.

As Andrew emerges from the courthouse, Tobias, still beside my car, calls out to him, 'Your sisters are over there!'

I find this unnerving. This is his first day in court: how does he know who we are?

I am getting daily early-morning calls on my cellphone. When I answer, there is a click and then silence. I grow increasingly paranoid, convinced I am being stalked. I ring the tall, avuncular police inspector who has replaced Bailey. He calls me 'my darling' and assures me that the calls are unlikely to be connected to the trial. I turn my phone to silent and stop answering it.

The following day, a very large, very dark man appears in the witness box. Speaking with a strong French accent, he identifies himself as Sebastiaan Vyabandi, the owner of a nightclub called Club Jazzay, which is opposite Mr Burger in Voortrekker Road. He knows both Chris and Ernest Arendse, he says.

Vyabandi says his clients have been complaining about the bouncers roughing them up, so he decided to spend the night outside the club to check it out for himself. At about 2 a.m., he saw Tobias get out of the front passenger seat of the Mercedes with an object in his hands. It was my father's camera, a high-end film Nikon, still in its case, which also contained a detachable long lens and wide-angle lens.

Vyabandi says Tobias had assured him it was not stolen, producing from the case a receipt for £400. This rings a bell. My brother had bought the camera for my

The trial

father while on a trip to London. This, apparently, was enough to convince Vyabandi and he brokered the sale to one of his customers.

Again, I feel I am being asked to enter an alternate reality, constructed of myths and half-truths. Vyabandi may well be an upstanding citizen but the milieu in which he operates is murky. I am reminded of Caryn Dolley's *The Enforcers: Inside Cape Town's Deadly Nightclub Battles*, which tells how the nightclub bouncer trade is controlled by the gangs. Bouncers are linked to the extortion of businesses and to drug peddling in clubs. And quite possibly also the fencing of stolen goods.

Meanwhile, forensic evidence on Tobias's and Thomas's clothes has come back. It is not clear why it took so long for DNA testing to be done on their clothing; this is more than two years after the murder. And it proves to be the most damning evidence against Thomas: both my father's blood and his own were found on one of his socks, taken as evidence by the police on the night of the arrest.

Tobias was in the clear – the blood on his jeans and takkies was not my father's. It told of an act of violence, but not the one that involved my father.

On 10 November, more than a month into the trial, Cecil Thomas himself takes the stand. Looking straight at my brother and sister and me, he says that he is very sorry for what happened to my father and the pain it has caused. He does not, however, take any responsibility for it.

He persists with his story that he had been set up by Tobias and the two other unnamed men, who had threatened to kill his family and him unless he found a buyer for the Mercedes.

Thomas speaks softly in Afrikaans and with a bad stutter so it is difficult to make out what he is saying. But what is clear is that he is yet again changing his story in an attempt to counter the evidence that has been presented by the witnesses for the state.

He concedes that he wasn't, as he had originally told the police, picked at random by the gangsters in Saron. Instead, he says, he bumped into Tobias at Bellville Railway Station on the weekend before the murder. He has known Tobias since 2004, he says, when they met at a dance hall in Bellville. Later, they frequently smoked tik together in Ernest Arendse's tik house above Mr Burger. Tobias is lying when he says he doesn't know the Tulbagh area – he makes deliveries of tik to Tulbagh, Gouda and Ceres, nearby towns, so he knows the area well.

When they met at Bellville Station, he mentioned to Tobias that he had heard there might be a job as a boilermaker in Worcester, a larger town about eighty-five kilometres southeast of Saron in the Western Cape interior, which he wanted to explore. Tobias offered to give him a lift to Worcester; they agreed to meet in front of the Spar in Tulbagh on the afternoon of Monday 11 August. He got a lift in from Saron and met Tobias as arranged. Tobias then introduced him to two men sitting in the car.

The trial

Asked to identify the men or describe them, Thomas refuses. He does, however, reveal that they acknowledged each other with a prison gang greeting: '*Hosh, hulle is die brasse van Bellville* ('Hosh, they are the brothers from Bellville').

Once Thomas had located the house, all four of them drove up to a 'beauty spot', a viewing point, outside Tulbagh where they drank beer and Klipdrift brandy, and smoked tik. It was here, claims Thomas, that he first heard of their real goal: they knew that the *argitek* had money in his house and they were going to do a *nommer*. He begged them to take him home to Saron first but the men said that if he failed to cooperate, they would kill him, and they would also kill his mother and his children. He believed them, he says, because they were gangsters.

When it got dark, they drove down into the town and parked in Buitenkant Street, which runs along the bottom of my father's garden. In an attempt to explain away the fact that my father's blood was found on his sock, Thomas claims he was forced to remove all his clothing and swap it with that of one of the unnamed men.

Tobias and the other man went into the house, returning periodically with bloodied hands and black rubbish bags, which they stuffed into the boot. Thomas remained in the car with a gun to his head, held by the driver, who locked the doors so he couldn't escape. When the men returned from the house for the last time, they gave him back his clothes, including the bloodied sock, and made him put them on.

His explanation for the two calls made to his friend's phone in Saron from my father's phone while the attack was underway is that one of the gangsters had brought the phone out to the car and told him to phone the number given and simply say four words: '*Ek het die kluise.*' ('I have the safes.')

Thomas complains that, at the station, DI Bailey had taken him to a room upstairs and said, '*Jy moet die fokken waarheid vertel, jou ma se poes!*' ('Tell the truth, motherfucker!')

The officer threw him to the floor. Another sat on his back and choked him, and then beat him with a sjambok. An examination by a district surgeon established that he had indeed been assaulted. Bailey took him to Karl Bremer Hospital, a state hospital in Bellville. There he was given painkillers, but the sister on duty said there was no need for further treatment.

Tobias, who was beaten up during the same interrogation, was more seriously injured. One of his legs had been broken.

Normally, I would have been appalled by this evidence of police violence. Now, I think, I'm glad they beat the shit out of the fuckers.

I have been studiously taking notes, trying to resurrect a professional self in an attempt to distance my personal self. But it doesn't work. I am too emotionally bound up with the victim. The bond with my father was particularly intense during the past few years as my mother slowly slipped away, leaving only a mute and helpless shell of herself behind. When she died, there was loss and grief and then the brave, tentative steps towards renewal. I had become so attuned to my father's emotional wavelength that the fact that I wasn't there to comfort him during the terror and pain of his final hours felt like a dereliction of duty, an abandonment.

In this low, depressed state, I find it difficult to sustain anger. The full weight of our country's brutal past weighs on me. I know little of Saron, except that it was originally established by German missionaries as a refuge for slaves.

Throughout my childhood, I remember overhearing my father repeatedly pronouncing to dinner guests, 'In five years' time, the blacks will rise up and drive us into the sea.' Rightly so, was the implication. The time scale never changed: it was always five years. So I grew up with a sense of precariousness, of looming retribution, always just beyond the horizon. I wonder if this conviction of my father's contributed, somehow, to his death – if, at some unconscious level, he invited his murderer in.

He moved to Tulbagh from a remote farm where he'd got into the habit of keeping substantial amounts of cash to pay his workers. In his new home, he secured two safes to the wall in his bedroom. In them, he kept some cash and two revolvers. During the renovations, with the constant procession of workmen through the house, he must, at some stage, have been careless about checking to see if anyone was around when he opened the safes. Someone must have seen the contents.

The cash was never recovered, and it was never clear how much of it there actually was. I thought it couldn't have been more than a few thousand rand, plus bits and pieces of foreign currency.

Standing on the steps of the courthouse one lunchtime, going over the evidence with Advocate Tshoele, I say, 'There couldn't have been a lot of money. Not more than R10 000.'

'That is a lot of money to most people,' she says gently.

3

In the cane fields

The court adjourns for a few days to give the judge and his assessors time to consider their verdict, and during that brief respite, I find myself thinking a lot about my father's fears. What was the basis of this conviction of his, that white people's nemesis awaited them and that it would arrive in bloody, chaotic form?

I think it started in Glendale, the sugar estate in a hot, sweet valley in northern Natal we moved to in the late sixties.

My father was in his late thirties, with a swatch of thick black hair and pale Scottish skin. We lived in Glendale for eight years, the longest stretch in my peripatetic childhood. Till then, we had moved every few years, when my father got fed up with his boss or his internal demons got too rowdy.

Glendale was owned by a prominent Muslim family,

the Paruks, based in Durban. In the late sixties apartheid was viciously enforced and it was unusual for an Indian family to own such an enterprise and for a white man to have an Indian boss. It was coincidental but fortuitous that the man to whom my father answered understood the affliction of volatile, seesawing moods.

As a child, I knew only that you had to stay out of my father's way when he was in a bad mood, which manifested in a snappy irritability and long periods of withdrawal when he lay on his bed and read, and was not to be disturbed.

One of the perks of my father's position as managing director was a house built to his specifications. It was a long, narrow bungalow perched high on the hill, just below the Paruks' grander house, with a panoramic view down to the mill on the banks of the thick, brown Umvoti River and the sugar cane fields that covered the surrounding hills like corn rows on a head. At one end of the house was his and my mother's suite – a bedroom, bathroom and small lounge – which we children were discouraged from entering. Right at the other end, beyond the kitchen and laundry, was a large playroom, our domain.

My parents' politics were liberal. My father was proud of the fact that he had been present at the formation of the Progressive Party. He hated the National Party and the policies it enforced. We were brought up to treat everyone with respect, no matter their race or class.

Nevertheless, he found himself in a business that

embodied a rigidly stratified racial hierarchy.

Below our house, in descending order of management hierarchy, were those of the other white staff: the engineer, the field manager, the mill manager, the electrician. At the bottom of the hill, on the banks of the river, was the modest housing where the Hindi-speaking employees who did the semi-skilled jobs lived with their families. There was a school and a community hall. Dotted all over the hills were the thatched wattle-and-daub homes where the amaZulu lived.

At the very bottom of the hierarchy were the amaMpondo, who were bussed down from the Eastern Cape for a few weeks every year to do the toughest job, the harvesting of the cane. It was done manually then, and they worked in the blazing heat, colourful bandanas wrapped around their foreheads to keep the sweat out of their eyes, the glaring sun glinting off their pangas as they lifted them high and then swung them into the rigid, fibrous cane.

The amaMpondo, who came without their families, were housed in a stark, grey compound near the road that led to Stanger, the nearest town, where we went to school. A bus would pick us up each morning and wind its way through the valley up to the main road linking the interior to the town. The road was gravel, potholed and bumpy. The journey took an hour each way. On the rare occasion when we got decent rain, the Umvoti spilled into the road and it became impassable, trapping us in the valley.

For us children, this was heaven. The entire mill and its surrounding estates were our playground. We would hack off pieces of cane, slice off the bark and then suck on the sweet fibres as we made our way down the hill to the mill. There, we would fish in the dam with homemade rods after stopping off at the Indian shop to buy sweets. The Indian shop was an Aladdin's cave of exotica – beads and paraffin lamps, colourful lengths of cloth and blankets hanging from hooks. Most enticing of all were the large glass jars of different sweets on the counter. The shopkeeper would count them out for us – 'Four Chappies bubblegum, six orange balls, four humbugs …' – till all our pocket money was used up. We had terrible teeth.

We all look back on Glendale as a golden period. It was a time of freedom and wildness and a symbiotic connection with nature, so dependent were we on its whims and caprices.

Glendale was on the wrong side of the mountain for rain, and my father's job was to increase the harvest in spite of this. One night the rain bucketed down for the first time in months, and my father and I ran out onto the front lawn, soaking our clothes and hair.

I remember phone calls in the dead of night, after which my father would dash out of the house and be gone for hours, arriving back at dawn, exhausted and smelling of smoke. In the hot, dry air, a wildfire could devour acres of cane in a flash. There was no fire service to rely on. Employees would have to be roused and transported to the scene – beaters frantically slapping at flames, water collected manually from the Umvoti and sprayed from hoses.

My father orchestrated all this, roaring backwards and forwards on winding dirt roads in his doughty Mercedes. I think he found it exhilarating, the drama of it, the tangible subduing of the foe. It was only the next day, when light exposed the extent of the damage – the loss of crops, blackened sticks of cane whittled to nothing, the juicy sweetness within sucked dry – that the low would come. The recognition that this year's harvest would fall below expectation, and that he would miss his target.

My father was brought up Anglican. My mother, with Irish roots, was a devout Catholic. At my grandmother's insistence, they were married in a Catholic church, where my father had to promise to bring their children up Catholic. What he hadn't anticipated was how quickly and prolifically they would arrive. My mother's only concession to contraception was the rhythm method, a Russian roulette of a system that required abstention from sex on the days when she was fertile. Maths was never her strong point, and by the time she was 30 and my father 31, they'd had five children.

The next pregnancy was an ectopic one, which nearly killed her. We were on holiday down the south coast with my grandparents when she started writhing in agony. My father rushed her to hospital, where it was revealed that the foetus had ruptured her fallopian tube and that she had peritonitis. Doctors removed both tubes and her womb. No more babies.

Our week was punctuated by the rituals of faith: catechism on Monday, confession on Friday and mass on Sunday. The last worked in my father's favour. At 6 a.m., my mother would haul the five of us out of bed and shepherd us, breakfastless and thirsty, into her Peugeot station wagon. She would drive us up out of the valley to Stanger, where the nearest Catholic church was. Here, we would endure an hour of staggering tedium – mass was still said in Latin then – until the final 'amen', when we'd burst out into the sunlight. One of the good ladies of the parish would then invite us home for tea and sandwiches before the long journey home. This would give my father a clear three hours of blissful, child-free silence.

But a slow revolt was burning in my mother: she began to resent her years of endless pregnancies and the toll they had taken on her body.

My father built a clinic on the banks of the Umvoti and every Monday my mother would drive her battered Peugeot into Durban and come back laden with bags of mielie meal, lentils and powdered milk.

On Wednesdays, the clinic would open and Zulu women would come down from the hills, babies strapped to their backs, to consult the doctor, who drove in from Stanger. During school holidays, my sister and I would help out, playing with the babies and dispensing the food my mother had bought.

With the zeal of the newly converted, she also began to dish out birth-control pills to the mothers who came to the clinic. I doubt they took them. This was my mother's crusade – other women should not have to endure what she had. On this count, at least, the church was wrong.

When I think back to our time in Glendale, it seemed to me – and this may be coloured by the rosy lens of nostalgia – stress-free in terms of crime: there wasn't any. The freedom allowed to us children was proof of that. We roamed wherever we wanted and often it was miles from the house. Neither parent ever tried to keep tabs on us. There were no burglar bars or alarms. We had a token watchman, who arrived each evening after dark, swathed in a large, khaki coat, whatever the weather, carrying a knobkerrie made of some dark wood, its rounded top highly polished. The watchman dozed beside the coal stove that theoretically heated the water for the house – it was seldom more than lukewarm – and as dawn rose he would walk back down the hill.

My father did have guns, though – mostly rifles. He kept them locked in a special cupboard in his and my mother's bedroom. We were each allocated one. He set up a clay pigeon cannon on the hill above the house and we would take turns to miss the arcs that spun high in the air before crashing into the cane fields. Only Guy and my dad were any good. But I did learn to clean a rifle and eventually even managed to hit a few clay pigeons.

Life may have been good for us, but it wasn't for everyone. Maybe my father was more aware than we were of subterranean rumblings and the possibility of eruption. Maybe this explained the cupboard full of rifles, which only appeared after we had moved to Glendale.

Very early one Saturday, we were woken by Guy pounding up the passage to my parents' room, shouting, 'Dad, Dad, the *impis* are here!'

His was the only room that faced the back yard. We rushed in, to be met by an extraordinary sight: thirty or so men, naked to the waist, standing in formation, as if posing for a photo, gazing unblinking back at us. The thing that was most eerie was that they were completely silent.

My father sprang into action, ordering all of us to their room on the other side of the house. From there we heard his voice, urgent, anxious, on the phone to the field manager. Through my parents' window, we watched the field manager's bakkie screech up our driveway. Shortly afterwards, the workers started filing down the driveway in twos and threes, threat and fear dissipated.

Dad explained that they were dissatisfied with their wages and living conditions, and had come to the house because they wanted to talk to the boss – not to the field manager, who wasn't listening to them.

A few days later, early one evening, he returned home with a huge, livid bruise on the underside of his arm. He had driven into the yard of the amaMpondo compound, he explained, and wound down his window because he wanted to talk to the men himself. A half-brick had come flying through the window. He had lifted his arm just in time to block it from smashing into his face.

I think it was the following year, when the amaMpondo were again to be seen in the cane fields, slashing at the cane, that a panicky call came one night. The amaMpondo were rioting. The mill building was on fire.

The gun cupboard was unlocked; the rifles were bundled up and put into the car. My father sped off, shouting at my mother to keep us all locked in the bedroom and to expect the wives and children of other white employees to join us in our large house at the top of the hill.

Much of what transpired that night was kept from us, but I garnered from low, tense conversations between my parents that the mill watchman had been murdered in the riot, his head slashed from his body. I thought of the gentle, silent man who kept watch over us every night and prayed it wasn't him.

4

The verdict

The judge is damning in his summing up: Cecil Thomas is a liar, he says. He cannot remember when he last came across a witness who changed his story so glibly every time new evidence challenged the existing one.

The clothes-swapping story is nonsense, as is his claim to have been kept in a car at gunpoint. Thomas murdered my father and he made the calls from his phone while in the house.

One thing the judge is not sure of is whether Thomas acted alone. This, however, does not affect his verdict: Thomas is guilty of murder and aggravated robbery.

A great cry arises from the benches behind us, followed by loud sobbing. It seems his family believed that he would be declared innocent.

Thomas's niece has flown out from London, where she is working as a carer, to attend the trial. After the

The verdict

verdict is handed down, she takes the stand to give evidence in mitigation of sentence. She explains that Cecil Thomas is the youngest of 10 children and her mother is the eldest, so she and Cecil were about the same age and grew up together.

Weeping, she begs the judge not to impose a harsh sentence. Her uncle is a good man *'wie net een fout gemaak het'* ('who made only one mistake'). A pretty big mistake, I think bitterly, but I am nevertheless struck by the depth of her grief and her love for the man. Her uncle had big dreams, she says, one of which was to move with his family to Australia, where his welding and boilermaking skills were prized. Those dreams, she cries, died today in this courtroom. What goes through my mind is, If only he had buggered off to Australia.

On 22 November 2010, the judge pronounces sentence. Describing my father as 'a good man' whose motivation for his lifelong campaign against the concentration of wealth was its effect on poor people, he can, the judge says, be considered an 'activist for the underprivileged'.

But it is not just the nature of the victim that he has to consider when determining the sentence, says the judge, but the effect on the community. The murder itself and the exceptional brutality involved has to be seen in a wider context.

Looking directly at Thomas, he says, 'You are probably too young to realise where we come from; how, as a community, we were broken and driven apart as a result of the system [of apartheid]. We are trying now to build a nation and one of the biggest threats to our democracy is crime. We stand, Mr Thomas, for the promotion of humanity and this type of crime threatens that. I talk of the community and of the nation because that is how serious it is. It is in all our interest to create a safe and humane society where we can live together with mutual respect.'

Nevertheless, he says, in considering an appropriate sentence for Thomas, he has to demonstrate the same humanity. The state asked for a life sentence and his initial inclination was to grant one.

However, after much consideration of the 'human material' standing before him, he has decided to give him a chance to change his life. He believes Thomas is salvageable and has chosen to give him a chance to reform. He will impose not a life sentence, but one that would allow for parole after a certain minimum has been served. Thus, it is in Thomas's own hands when he will be free again.

The judge points out – and this is something that puzzles me too – that Thomas does not fit the mould of a gangster murderer. He has no history of violent crime and has never been to prison. He has been nurtured by a loving, supportive family and is relatively well educated, with a highly marketable skill.

'Something happened to you in August 2008, or before that. Maybe drugs. Maybe the influence of others. Because others must have been involved.' He looks

The verdict

directly at Thomas. 'There is something you are not telling us.

'I can't find that you repented what you had done. You're sorry but it is yourself you are sorry for. A big limitation is: what actually happened? And why? I don't know the answer to that. I can only speculate. This incident appears totally out of character – this is why I wonder whether I have heard the full story.'

I expected a life sentence – all the evidence seems to me to point to premeditated murder. But the judge sentences Thomas to 25 years for the murder and another 15 for aggravated theft, 10 of which are to run concurrently. He will be eligible for parole halfway through an effective 30 years.

During the trial, Advocate Tshoele suggests only half-jokingly that I visit my father's grave and attempt to talk to him the way she talks to her ancestors. Ask him what happened in that house, she urges. I wish I can, because only he and his murderer know what happened in that final hour of his life. And he is dead, and the murderer is not telling.

I walk out of the court for the last time feeling utterly drained. There is a sense of exhaustion, coupled with a deep relief that I will never have to sit in that courtroom again. But there remains the jaggedness of unfinished business. The trial has been a blur of what felt like selective truths. Too much new information came at me to take in and cohere into a narrative that feels authentic. I am too numbed to absorb it properly and too frightened to fully internalise it in a way that makes sense to me.

As I drive home, almost unconsciously I try out a technique a psychologist friend has recommended: I put it all in an imaginary box and let the box drift into the ether. It is still there, bobbing above me, but I resolve that it will no longer consume me.

The murderer – or murderers – have already taken too much from me. I have to move on now and get on with my life.

5

Bastard fate strikes again

And get on with my life I do. My first task is to get off the drugs. I associate the chemicals that clog my brain and pad my body with fat with my suffering self, a self I am now desperate to slough off.

When I first started taking them, I was willing to shove anything down my throat. Now, for the first time, I do a Google search on the drugs I have been swallowing for the past couple of years. Seroquel, I discover, is a heavy-hitter – an antipsychotic used to treat major disorders like schizophrenia and bipolar disorder.

Side effects include 'significant weight gain'. I give myself a couple of weeks as a weaning-off period, taking one every other day and then every third day, and flush the remainder down the loo.

Within a couple of months, I shed not only the 10 kilograms I have put on, but a couple more besides. I also lose the ability to sleep, dropping off at 2 a.m. and waking at 4 a.m. My anxiety levels rocket. I go back to my GP, who prescribes zolpidem. Half a tablet at night and I plunge into a deep and dreamless unconsciousness for five or six hours. The anxiety is still there, but at a muted level. I feel my energy and drive returning.

Little do I suspect that fate hasn't finished with me.

But, for now, life begins to feel liveable again.

I plunge myself into work, always my saviour.

In 2011 I undertake another rugby book, which entails spending several weeks with the Springboks in New Zealand with the aim of producing an intimate, blow-by-blow account of how our boys manage to bring home the Rugby World Cup. Given the passionate attachment to rugby among South Africa's book-buying classes, I hope to make my fortune. But the Boks are ignominiously bounced out of the tournament in the quarterfinals and the book turns out to be less a record of triumph than an anatomy of failure, which doesn't exactly ignite the sales charts.

I am, at the same time, working on another book. Medecins Sans Frontières asks me to help create an accessible account of the struggle for universal access to antiretrovirals at the turn of the 21st century when HIV/Aids was cutting a swathe through the population. It is a heartening story to tell: how civil society worked together to defeat both the protectionism of Big Pharma and the inexplicable denialism of then president Thabo Mbeki to defeat the Aids monster that was gobbling up lives that should have flourished with the arrival of democracy.

This is not my first foray into the challenging world of HIV/Aids. In 2005, at the height of the epidemic, I wrote a book about the eventful life and premature, agonising Aids death of an iconic post-apartheid DJ. It became a bestseller, prescribed in university anthropology and creative non-fiction classes and used by NGOs for HIV/Aids education. It was a difficult book to write, drenched with grief and pain. The Medecins Sans Frontières story feels like an antidote.

From my flat on the Atlantic Seaboard, I have easy access to some of the most magical parts of Cape Town. I take long walks along the promenade edging the Atlantic Ocean and swim in the salty Sea Point pool. Lying on my back doing lazy backstroke to counter the hours spent crouched over a computer, I gaze up at Lion's Head while waves crash against the pool's edge.

And love comes flying in, out of the blue. Alan and I first met as undergraduates at UCT, a million years ago. Our meeting again is the stuff of fairy tales. Our eyes lock across a crowded ballroom one hot January night.

The venue is the majestic Mount Nelson Hotel, the occasion the launch of a book by a former British ambassador, Robin Renwick. It is a grand, if sweaty, affair – the air conditioning has broken down. I was invited because Renwick and I shared a publisher. Alan is there courtesy of his political pedigree. The attraction was immediate – and lasting.

A couple of days later, we meet for a long, windy walk on the Sea Point Promenade. Huge swells batter the sea wall, flicking salty spray over us. It feels to me in my exalted state like the christening of a rebirth. We talk non-stop, catching up on the lives we have each lived in the intervening decades. I tell him about my years abroad, first as a freelance reporter in South Korea and then on *The Guardian* in London. I tell him about my joy at being home. I don't mention my father.

While I was overseas, Alan immersed himself in the heady project of refashioning our country into a democratic state. A developmental economist, he was a senior member of the team working first with Nelson Mandela and then with Thabo Mbeki to transform the country from an isolationist, white-supremacist state into a modern, thriving, democratic one. I think wistfully, as he talks, that I missed out on those years.

By the time Jacob Zuma came to power, Alan was head of economic policy in the presidency. Within a couple of years, it became clear that Zuma had a very different agenda from those of his predecessors, so Alan returned to our alma mater with a different mission.

If South Africa is to survive this period, he explains, it needs capable, ethical public servants. And so he set up, from scratch, the Nelson Mandela School of Public Governance, a postgraduate school for young leaders from all over Africa.

I am in awe of what he has achieved. This is a good man, a decent man. What he also reveals is an emotional rawness. He is newly out of a long marriage. We agree to take it slowly.

He rents a flat down on the beachfront, a twenty-minute walk down the hill from my place. His flat has a large balcony overlooking the Sea Point swimming pool and on summer evenings we eat there, with seagulls soaring, squawking, over us. We watch flotillas of kayaks float by and container ships queuing up outside Cape Town harbour. If we are lucky, we see dolphins and whales.

In 2014, the year in which Alan and I meet up again, the country is in trouble. I have never subscribed to my father's view of an approaching apocalypse, forever just over the horizon. I see our country instead as a work in progress, slowly but surely jolting towards a just and sustainable future. One step back, two steps forward.

As Jacob Zuma's presidency progresses, however, the rhythm changes. The steps backwards became larger and faster. Thabo Mbeki's Aids blind spot notwithstanding, he presided over a golden period in post-apartheid history, the steady building of a mostly ethical, modern state. Under Zuma, this is being hollowed out. A substantial section of the ANC is revealed as being profoundly corrupt and under Zuma they are being given free rein to loot public coffers.

The effects are felt everywhere: corruption in the secret service and the police make South Africa a less safe place to be. The economy shrinks and the extensive welfare state built up under Mandela and Mbeki is under threat. Welfare grants are critical to lifting millions of people out of poverty – and helping to narrow the yawning chasm between the rich (mostly white) elite and the poor black majority. By early 2017, Zuma's kleptocratic grip appears unshakeable.

Leadership in general is poor. Some twenty years into democracy, the political landscape is still skewed along racial lines.

Neither does the official opposition offer hope. Cape Town, where we live, is run efficiently by the main opposition party, the Democratic Alliance. But for different reasons – which are mainly about appeasing their core funders and voters, who are wealthy, white and myopic – they have left the apartheid-era racial and class structure largely intact.

Despairing of the mainstream parties but feeling the need to do something, I begin volunteering at an NPO that provides support for township-based activists working to improve education, safety and housing.

One particular job stands out. I am asked to organise a press conference to highlight how the lack of security measures in schools in gang-infested townships is affecting children. The venue is a primary school in Nyanga.

Initially established as a dormitory town for black workers, Nyanga occupies just over three square kilometres, and is distinguished by the fact that it has the highest proportion of murders in the world. It is one of the oldest black townships in South Africa, built to house African people moved from their homes in the centre of Cape Town during apartheid. To get there, I drive down the N2, past the airport, for 26 kilometres. It drive feels further, so different is it from the calm, ordered city I have just left: the roads are full of potholes, some traffic lights don't work, and cars – especially minibus taxis – don't always heed those that do. Pedestrians and vendors weave in and out of traffic.

Lining the road to the entrance to the school is a row of chop shops masquerading as repair shops, where men labour over the skeletons of stolen cars. Around them are stacked their entrails – engines, tyres, gearboxes, batteries and hubcaps. Sparks fly from welding torches. I drive through open school gates, park and walk in.

I am surprised by how large and solid the school is – long, low buildings built in rectangles around grassed courtyards. But there is an eerie, abandoned feeling to it, and not just because it is 2 p.m. and classes are over for the day. In a suburban school, there would be games and sport, teachers and parents hovering.

Two little boys in grey shorts and crisp white shirts appear, asking in careful English, 'How are you?' Their little faces beam delight at the sight of a stranger. Insisting on helping me with my bags – laptop, camera, notebook – they walk solemnly alongside me to the principal's office.

At the press conference, the principal – a courteous woman with an air of endurance – explains that the chop shops outside the school gates work with the gangs, gutting stolen cars to sell the parts or reconstituting them to disguise their origins. Despite the fact that criminals dominate the turf outside the school gates, the City of Cape Town provides no security. There is no way to lock the gates. There are no security guards. Sometimes, rival gangs stage shootouts in the school grounds. Teachers and children have to lie on the floor to avoid getting struck by stray bullets. 'We call the police but they don't come,' she says. Only one journalist turns up.

A mother tells how gangsters openly peddle drugs to children on their way to school and try to recruit them. Most parents don't have cars – even small children must walk to school.

I drive home, my valuables hidden in the boot, car windows closed and doors locked, feeling a familiar sense of despair and impotence.

And then, in July of 2017, fate strikes another body blow. With Zuma looking increasingly entrenched, another of the NPOs with which I work organises a public meeting to discuss how best to support the gathering momentum towards his impeachment.

On the day in question, we have been setting up the hall where the meeting is due to take place when we realise we need a register of those who attend so that we can invite them to future meetings. I have just the thing at home so I nip back at lunchtime to pick it up. As I drive up the steep driveway of the complex in which I live, I see that a black Polo is blocking the entrance to my garage. Irritated, I park nearby, walk up to the car and knock on the window. A young white guy is dozing, his seat reclined. He starts awake and winds down the window. 'Please don't park in front of my garage,' I say curtly and walk back down the hill to my flat.

Within seconds, I feel a tremendous force bashing into me from behind. I turn to see a black car looming over me. I feel a further blow, against my side, knocking me to the ground. In that split second it comes to me that if I don't react, the car will keep going and it will mow me down and crush me.

I start screaming. The car stops. I find myself on my hands and knees. Dazed with shock, still screaming, I look down at my left hand, at the end of a long black sleeve. It seems to be too far from my body: disproportionately so, a pale, spiky thing, flat against the tarmac. I can't feel or move my left arm. There is blood everywhere. It seems to me that my arm has been severed from my body. In that second, a shadow swoops over me, blotting out the sunlight. This is death, I think, come to get me, as it had my father.

My neighbours appear. They help me into a car and rush me to the Cape Town Mediclinic. Over the next couple of hours, I learn that my left shoulder is dislocated – the ball cracked – and the bones of my upper arms shattered. The left side of my head and face is badly bruised and there are deep abrasions on my hands and knees. The injuries are severe, but I will live.

Later, I tell Alan about the black shadow. It was probably a hang-glider, he says gently, on its way to the promenade from Signal Hill.

Of course, I think, feeling silly.

My shoulder and arm are reassembled with a bone graft, a plate and several screws. After the surgery, the surgeon, tall, gangly and startlingly young, appears at my bedside: 'It's going to be a long haul,' he says. Still heavily drugged, I have no idea then what he means.

I soon find out. For the first weeks, I am dependent on others for the most intimate tasks and in constant, intense pain as bones, ligaments, nerves and muscles heal and knit. But most debilitating is a sense of panic that I cannot budge. I am consumed by the thought that I almost died and that death still stalks me. As it was after my dad's murder and the trial, I lose all sense of personal safety. I am afraid to leave the flat. Travelling in a car leaves me shaking.

But this time, I feel anger. More than that: I feel a pure, blinding rage. The difference is this: as I later learnt, the man who knocked me down in my driveway was a young white man, a recovering alcoholic employed by one of Cape Town's many rehab centres for well-heeled addicts, both local and foreign. When I disturbed his nap, he was waiting for a fellow addict who lives in our complex.

These two are white, middle-class: privileged, in other words. I feel they have absolutely no excuse. I have increasingly lurid fantasies of watching both die slowly and painfully from an overdose. I see the addict frequently – and the man who knocked me down continues to visit him. Neither ever approaches me to apologise or ask after my welfare.

Neighbours called the police at the time of the accident but they failed to pitch up. When I go to file a report at the police station after I am discharged from hospital, the police say there is nothing they can do because the accident happened in a private space. This seems implausible – if he killed me, would there still be no recourse? – but I don't have the strength to argue.

Although it feels like it, I am not marked out in any way. In 2008, the year my father died, 18 479 others were murdered in South Africa. In 2017, the year I was injured by a car in my driveway, 14 050 people were killed in traffic accidents.

I am not immune to the consequences of everyday violence, but I am better placed than many to deal with them. I receive the best possible support, operated on by a specialist surgeon in a private hospital with all the post-operative care I need.

My family rally round. Alan is in the UK teaching a course at the London School of Economics, so when I'm admitted to the hospital I ask my neighbour to call Guy. He and Liza immediately leave Betty's Bay, where they live, and drive the hour and a half into Cape Town. They deal with the admissions process, consult with the surgeon and bring me nightclothes and toiletries.

The next morning, Cathy and her daughter, Anna, wait outside the operating theatre for the three hours it takes to put my shoulder and arm back together again, and take me home when I am discharged, staying with me until Alan can get back from London.

When he returns, he moves in with me. He does the shopping, cleaning and cooking. He looks after me with selfless tenderness, changing my dressings and accompanying me to doctor's appointments. If anything is needed to convince me how lucky I am to have found him, it is this.

Nevertheless, I struggle. Despite a steady supply of morphine, the pain jolts me awake every couple of hours and I get up, taking care not to disturb him, and pace around the dark flat, alternating between despair and rage.

This time, I find a cognitive behavioural therapist. It's a good choice: she is pragmatic and perceptive. It is classic post-traumatic stress disorder, she says. My brain went into panic mode at the time of the accident and hasn't relinquished it. The alarm that went off then is still ringing. I am still on constant high alert for disaster.

Naming it helps but it doesn't make it go away. I am convinced that I cheated death but that it is coming for me, and that next time I won't survive.

Night after night, as I pace the flat, unable to sleep because of the pain, it floods over me: the shock of the murder; the unfolding horror of the trial. I am right back where I was when Cecil Thomas was led out of the court for the last time.

This time, though, I am not numbed by drugs. The shock and grief rage through every crackling circuit in my brain. I become obsessed with the thought that I have to track Cecil Thomas down and force him to tell me what happened. Before it is too late and death catches up with me.

And then dawn rises, pink and hopeful, over the shimmering sea and my dark thoughts shrivel and retreat. I come up with a plan. I will make this pain bearable by telling a story about it.

Excited, I pour it all out when next I see my therapist. She is not encouraging. Firstly, she says, I am in no condition to take on the trauma of confronting Thomas. Secondly, she says, imposing a narrative on the experience will be my way of imposing control, thereby blotting out feelings that should be explored in a gentle and safe space. Like her consulting rooms.

But I have always written my way out of despair. Simply recording and describing how I am feeling, and why, has always proven cathartic and shown me a way forward. I am aware, though, that this is of a different order from anything I hve ever tried to articulate before. I am going to have to venture into very dark territory.

As soon as I have this thought, it is followed by another: things can't get any worse than they are already. All my certainties, my illusions of safety, have been shattered. One of the consequences of my father's murder and my assault that is particularly unsettling is the realisation of how little control I have over what happens to me. That, no matter how you live your life, how responsible you try to be towards your fellow humans, how much you do to protect yourself, there is something out there that can destroy you in one fell swoop. I feel as if I am at the bottom of a deep pit, scrabbling around in the dark for a way out.

The despair begins to lift as I think my way through my new plan. I will explore my father's life and Thomas's, to the point where they collided.

I make one concession to my therapist. I will start with the easy bit: my father.

Exploring his life – and how it shaped ours – seems a gentle place to start.

6

Weaving it all together

If it wasna for the weavers what wad they do?
They wadna hae claith made oot o' oor woo',
They wadna hae a coat neither black or blue,
Ginit wasna for the work o' the weavers.
– *David Shaw, weaver and poet (1786-1856), published in 'Vagabond Songs and Ballads of Scotland' by Robert Ford'*

It is late November 2017, four months after my accident. Alan and I sit around a farmhouse kitchen table in a B&B in Stuartfield in northeastern Scotland. Stuartfield is not exactly tourist central, and the Millview B&B is the only accommodation available. The nearest restaurant is in the next town. You used to be able to get a meal at the pub, we are told, but it has now folded and all that's left of it is the sign dangling forlornly over a locked door.

Fiona, our landlady, has offered to make dinner for us and the only other guests, three English hunters. It has been dark since 3.30 p.m. but the room is bright and warm, courtesy of vigorous central heating and a monster of an Aga on which Fiona is cooking. At the far end of the room, Fiona's husband, fresh in from the fields, watches TV, a grandchild playing at his feet.

The hunters have been out in the rain all day, looking in vain for geese to shoot. Stamping about in the woods, rifles cocked, in the bracing cold has given them an appetite and they tuck into the haggis-stuffed chicken breasts and steaming boiled potatoes Fiona sets down before us. Alan, a foodie, will try anything once and gamely tackles the haggis. I ease mine out of the chicken and slide it onto his plate.

The older of the hunters, a bulky, ruddy-faced man, explains that he owns a manufacturing business in northwest England. The other two work for him: the hunt is a team-building exercise.

From the TV in the corner, a newsreader is talking about Brexit and I ask the older man what he thinks. He is a bit bemused by it, he says: he voted Leave, but on the assumption that it would be defeated. It was a protest vote because he was irritated by the pernickety EU rules by which his company must abide. He was as surprised as anyone when the Leavers beat the Remainers by four per cent. The two younger men nod vigorously at everything he says, adding brief affirmatory asides, chorus to the main act.

They ask, politely, how we feel about our president, Zuma, and Alan explains that he held a senior position in the president's office but quit shortly after Zuma arrived there. Enough said.

And you, he asks, turning to me. I am ancestor-hunting, I say. Ah, he says, we have all been there.

After dinner, they excuse themselves and head out into the night. This time, it is deer they are looking to kill.

We linger over our dessert, a homemade apple crumble served with thick yellow custard. Watching Fiona bustling about, I think about my impressions of the UK when I first arrived on these shores. In the mid-eighties, when apartheid seemed invincible and I, exhausted by the fight and longing for a glimpse of a bigger world, had booked a flight to London, with one large, unwieldy suitcase and a thousand pounds in traveller's cheques.

I remember the relief I felt at the weightlessness of my whiteness. The colour of my skin was not an instant identifier of a predator class. Still naïve as to the race and class dynamics of British society, I believed then that my colour attracted no unearned privilege or the insecurity and guilt that went with it.

I feel this again in that kitchen in northeastern Scotland. Fiona prepared our room earlier and is now loading the dishwasher and mopping the floor. A small, muscular woman in her early fifties with blonde hair scraped up in a bun, she is constantly on the go, seemingly unfazed by the endless series of chores that make up her day. In a similar establishment at home, a black woman would clean the toilets and wash the dishes while the white mistress issued instructions.

After dinner, I lie in a deep, hot bath, listening with pleasure to the rain battering the window. It means I don't have to feel guilty about the long baths I have been taking every night since we arrived. While I lie here, submerged up to my chin, the pain in my shoulder is but a bad memory and, weightless in the water, the joint glides easily through the mobilisation exercises urged on me by my physiotherapist. Through the open door I can see Alan lying on the bed reading in a halo of light from the bedside lamp.

At home in Cape Town, we are without the comfort of water. Swimming pools are closed. We are reduced to 30-second showers every other day. The house is scented by a lingering smell of urine. 'If it's yellow, let it mellow. If it's brown, flush it down.' The merry little jingle rings out at regular intervals from radio stations. The threat of Day Zero hangs over us: the day the taps run dry and we will have to queue at tankers to collect water rations.

Here, the exuberant burn has burst its banks and flooded the dirt road leading to the B&B. Overnight, new potholes emerge, filled with water. We edge our hire car over them gingerly, fearful of damaging it.

I pull out the plug and let some water gurgle out so that I can top up with hot water, and I mull over the visit I made that morning to what has become fixed in my mind as the McGregor ancestral home, a short walk away from the B&B.

On one side of the road is a dam. On the other, the house; two signs are attached to it. One says 'Waulkmill. The Dyesters'; the other, 'Quartalehouse'. I stand for a frozen moment in the rain, lost in a memory of a similar sign hanging beside the front door of another house in a hot, dry village.

For many years, my parents lived in a village on the edge of the Karoo. It was, coincidentally and much to my father's delight, called McGregor, one of the many towns and villages named for the Scots who flooded into South Africa around the turn of the century. Between 1893 and 1907, more Scots went to South Africa than to Australia, New Zealand or Canada. My father named their house in McGregor 'Quartalehouse'. I knew that this was related to my father's Scottish forebears but had little idea then of its significance in our history, or even how to pronounce it.

I see now that the original Quartalehouse is bounded by water: alongside the driveway to the north runs a bubbling burn. The dam feeds a stream that runs under the road and down the south side of the house. Once, it powered the giant mill wheel still affixed to the wall of the house, and the wool dyeing and bleaching business that three generations of the family ran here. It was this house and this life that Alexander McGregor, my great-grandfather, left behind when he travelled south to England and then to South Africa.

I have been here before. In the early nineties, my parents came to London to visit me and my father insisted we take this trip up to Scotland so that I could see where my family came from. He hired a car and off we set, stopping for a night in Edinburgh.

There is a photograph of my mother and father beside this sign and another of my mother and me. She is slim and elegant in a long, purple coat, borrowed from me. I am bulky in a voluminous down jacket, left over from two years in South Korea, where I had been freelancing for British newspapers. There is another picture of my mother laughing as she pretends to push the big wheel, towering above her.

The photographs are about all we took away from that visit. No one was home so we couldn't go inside. We had lunch in a nearby café and Dad asked the waitress if she knew anything about the McGregor mill. She looked blank, so we set off back to London after another night in Edinburgh.

I remember being slightly impatient with it all. I had recently got a staff job at *The Guardian* and I was discovering that my accent was an unexpected asset. It marked me as an outsider, and therefore not easily categorisable in an organisation dominated by the English elite, where branding was on the tongue rather than the skin. Being young and ambitious, I was not interested in my roots in a Scottish backwater.

This journey feels like a pilgrimage in my father's honour. He never managed to interest any of us in our Scottish heritage: our South Africanness was the only identity we wanted. Now, in my longing to recapture my father, I am in love with our fragment of Scottishness.

This gentle village seems so restful by comparison with the tortured, fractured country I have just come from. The last census recorded in Stuartfield shows that there are just 670 inhabitants, the vast majority of them born in Scotland, united by a common history and language. For 589 of them, English is their home language. Almost a tenth list Scots as their mother tongue. The only crimes recorded in contemporary Stuartfield are petty theft. You can safely walk the streets here – unless you freeze to death.

The family roots in this corner of northeastern Scotland are deep. Alexander was the third generation of McGregors born into Quartalehouse and the dyeing and bleaching business. In around 1810, his grandfather, John, had moved east to Stuartfield, one of the 'planned villages' that had sprung up in northeast Scotland in the late 1770s, where lairds sought to make money from their properties.

Stuartfield is named for the family that developed it: the Burnett-Stuarts. It's a pretty little village, flanked by two mills – the Milladen wool-spinning and carding mill at one end, and an oatmeal mill at the other.

Quartalehouse, between the two, was built to clean, bleach and dye the blankets woven at Milladen.

The textile industry is woven into the town's architecture: the heart of it is the town square, from which rows of 'houses and a half' branch off, the half being a small workroom where the family loom was housed. In Stuartfield's early days, most of its residents made their living from weaving.

The young couple who have just moved in are only the fourth owners of Quartalehouse. The husband commutes to his job in Aberdeen. Young families are attracted to Stuartfield: property is relatively cheap, there is a good primary school and, bordered by fields and burns, it offers clean air and easy access to nature.

Once I have explained my mission, the couple are warm and welcoming. I wander around the house trying to get a sense of what it must have been like when Alexander lived here. It feels now like a large and airy family house, just needing a few children to complete it. It's hard to imagine the packed, bustling space it must have been when my ancestors lived here.

A census count in 1881 – when Alexander was eight – showed that it housed twelve people: his parents and six siblings, plus a housemaid and two workers. There was a large washing machine where the rough wool lengths were washed before being cut to size. In the large garden was a shed where the blankets were whitened in a fug of steaming sulphur. On the upper level of the house, the blankets were finished – knots removed and stray threads sewn in. From a door that still leads directly to the road, the finished blankets were loaded onto horse carts and, later, lorries, to be taken to the warehouse.

The physicality of it – and its practical, enterprising nature – reminds me strongly of my father. After our return from Scotland, he and my mother spent a few nights with me in the West Hampstead flat I had just bought with the mortgage I had been able to obtain with my *Guardian* salary. It was a large, high-ceilinged, one-bed flat which backed on to a three-acre communal garden. It needed a lot of work, which delighted my father. He spent large amounts of time in the labyrinthine cellar of the Robert Dyas hardware store around the corner in Finchley Road, eventually leaving me with a cache of DIY tools extensive enough to start my own business – hich, of course, I never touched again. He put up shelves, replaced cracked tiles and assembled recalcitrant flatpack furniture. I still own the flat and the shelves he built still line the walls that flank the fireplace.

After taking my leave of the young couple, I walk through the village. My face, the only bit of me that is exposed, gradually becomes numb. In the churchyard I peer through the rain at mossy gravestones, searching for McGregors. The graveyard is enclosed by low stone walls, beyond which cows munch. A tumbling stream gurgles alongside. It's all very pretty but oh so cold!

By midday, I can't stand it any longer and walk back to the B&B. As I arrive, the hunters sweep up in a black

Land Rover, looking disgruntled. No luck. These creatures stay put when the weather is like this, mutters one.

Very wise. As we all should! I say cheerily. They don't respond.

Back at the B&B, Fiona is giving her oatmeal recipe to Alan, who has declared it the best oatmeal he has ever eaten. I wonder, watching them, whether this is how the McGregors would have ended up had they kept Quartalehouse: running a B&B for hunters – of both deer and ancestors.

It would certainly have been a safer life, but also a much smaller one.

7

Alexander and Nongoloza

The story my mother used to tell about Alexander was that while waiting to board his ship in Southampton, he'd got his landlady's daughter pregnant. Under pressure from said landlady, they hastily married and, in 1900, my great-aunt Dolly was born. Alexander must have stuck around for another couple of years because in 1902 another child came along: Robert, my grandfather.

Shortly afterwards, Alexander set sail for Durban, from where he took a train up to the goldfields on the Rand. He made periodic visits home but his wife, Margaret, and the two children remained in Kent. In 1920, shortly after the Great War ended, Margaret – a 'real battleaxe', according to my mother – got fed up with waiting for an invitation to join her husband and booked passages to South Africa for herself and their two children, then 18 and 20. My mother was not able to tell me whether they managed to live happily together but she had her doubts.

In my father's papers I found a photograph of the four of them, taken shortly after their reunion. Margaret, beak-nosed, stern-looking, has her arm around a young man whom at first I mistook for my father, so vivid was the likeness. But, of course, it is Robert, my grandfather, dapper in white trousers, shirt and shoes. Dolly, dark-haired like her brother, sits cross-legged at her mother's feet, leaning into her and smiling, squint-eyed, into the sun. Alexander has the posture of the proud paterfamilias: tall, square-shouldered, in jacket and tie, gazing, unsmiling yet benign, into the camera. But, tellingly, he stands behind and slightly apart from the others, not touching any of them. Margaret would have been 50 years old when the photograph was taken and Alexander 48.

In the last week of November, Alan flies home to Cape Town and I take the train south to Edinburgh, hot now on the trail of Alexander, questions fizzing in my mind. Why did he leave his comfortable life in Stuartfield? Why did he choose South Africa? Why did he leave his wife and children behind? And what, in the end, made him sever his ties with the land of his birth and throw in his lot with our turbulent country? Which, it seems, was not in the end particularly good for him,

From left: Robert, Margaret and Alexander with Susannah ('Dolly') at their feet

given that he didn't even make it to 60, while his father, back home in Scotland, lived to the ripe old age of 82.

For answers, I go first to the National Records Office on the Royal Mile, identifying it by the statue of Wellington rearing up on his horse, as if about to gallop triumphantly up the broad expanse of North Bridge stretching out before him. Under the horse's heels stands the red-clad figure of a Scottish Socialist Party worker, trying in vain to interest passersby in the dire straits of the working-class Scot.

I leave my backpack in a locker and make my way to the National Records Office where a librarian directs me to the original feu charter laying out the details of my family's claim to Quartalehouse.

John McGregor, it appears, has never owned it. Despite living and running his business from it all his adult life, he remained a tenant. It was only in 1910 that his son, Robert, was able to buy the feu – but it came with, well, feudal conditions. I find the original of the document, signed in Edinburgh on 18 May 1910, by which

> Eustace Robertson Burnett Stuart of Dens and Crichie granted Robert McGregor, dyer, of Quartalehouse, parish of Old Deer a feu charter to the dwelling house, byres, stable and other offices together with the waulkmill and outhouses. Bounded on the west by the road leading to the village of Old Deer, on the south by an overflow burn, on the east by a continuation of said

burn, known as Knockburn, and on the north and north west by a service road, with servitude right to use, for motive power, the water in the mill dam on the west side of the public road to Old Deer, and on the North West with the mill dam and mill lade connected therewith, valued at one hundred and sixty seven pounds, ten shillings and one penny sterling.

But this sum only entitled him to what was effectively a lease: Robert still had to pay a yearly feu duty to the Stuarts of £12. And, in the unlikely event that he were to find oil or gold underneath his property, it would belong to the Stuarts.

When Robert died 20 years later, he left Quartalehouse to Alexander. But Alexander had by then made his choice: from his new home at 77 Mansfield Road, Durban, he instructed solicitors to transfer the property to his sister, Jane. One of the witnesses was Elizabeth McGregor, also of Quartalehouse, a cousin of Jane's. It feels odd to see my own name, already embedded in family history way back when.

The next few days follow a happy pattern. After breakfast, which is cooked, served and cleared away virtually single-handedly by a young Polish woman, I set off over Calton Hill, along the Royal Mile and up to the National Library. It is perfect walking weather – the temperature hovers just above freezing but it is bright and dry. I lunch on soup and wholewheat bread in the canteen, and when the library closes at 7 p.m., I head out into the freezing dark, already lit up with sparkling Christmas markets strung out along the Royal Mile.

I stop for a bowl of pasta and a glass of red wine and then, swaddled in coat, woolly hat, scarves and gloves, I wander the streets, feeling echoes of the elation I felt when I arrived in the UK in the spring of 1985. For the first time in my life, I was able to walk alone up a dark street. How free and powerful it made me feel.

I spend a lot of time on those long, night-time walks pondering Alexander.

From my reading, I have begun to understand why he left. The Industrial Revolution siphoned off much of the industry from the villages of rural Scotland into the big weaving mills in the city. It was a dying way of life.

Two of his brothers emigrated to Canada at about the same time as he left for the goldfields, which, by then, were luring more Scots to South Africa than to any other British colony.

Perusing local newspapers from the period, it strikes me how intensively they covered the Boer War. Acres of newsprint were given over to detailed descriptions of skirmishes and manoeuvres. The Boers got a very bad rap and the motivation for the war – the desire of the British to get their hands on goldfields that promised huge riches – was barely mentioned. Little Stuartfield produced some volunteer soldiers and their accounts of their experiences on the 'veldt' were prominently displayed. Would this, I wonder, have influenced Alexander's decision to choose South Africa, and not Canada like his brothers?

What is more puzzling is his decision to leave his wife and children behind. Alexander came from a God-fearing, respectable family: abandoning Margaret and his unborn child would not have been an option. I wonder if this planting of his seed in home soil, on the verge of leaving it, was not an unconscious expression of ambivalence: a fearfulness of what might lie ahead and the looming loss of what he was leaving behind.

Such ambivalence has resonance for me. All my fertile years were swallowed up in long hours in the *Guardian* newsroom. I was always aware that if I had an English child with an English man I would be forever trapped there. I had seen it happen with South African friends. I preferred to remain uncommitted, one foot always out the door.

When I left South Africa in 1985, I was burnt out and exhausted. But, more than that, I yearned for a bigger, wider world than the one I had grown up in. As a white person, I felt trapped in an identity that felt tainted. Catholicism had taught me that I came into the world soiled with original sin. From my first holy communion at the age of five, weekly recounting a litany of sins to the invisible representative of an all-seeing God had reinforced a sense of always being morally on the back foot.

Alan and I joke about this – he is Jewish, so he knows all about ineradicable guilt. But his is at least confined to family and tribe. Catholics feel guilty about everything.

When I went to university at the age of 17, I swapped Catholicism for socialism and the anti-apartheid struggle. The stain of original sin became visible – the colour of my skin, all too clear a stamp of the oppressor.

In my second year at UCT, a hundred or so of us marched down Vanguard Drive to the townships in an attempt to throw in our lot with black students after the 1976 Soweto uprising. We were arrested and held overnight in jail. I remember the food: a thick slab of white margarine on tasteless white bread. A seat-less toilet in the middle of our communal cell and a single blanket so rough it grazed my skin. Alan was also arrested, but held in the men's section. We knew each other, but not well. He was tall and clever, with a mop of curly black hair, and seemed always to be flanked by a guard of fierce women. I was new to the left and wary of these seasoned warrior women.

My father was in court to bail me out, angry and frightened. But he paid my bail and took me to lunch at a fancy hotel when he realised how hungry I was. The whole thing had been a shock for him. He had barely slept the night before. He said he had been phoned and told I was in prison, but not which one, so he had gone from prison to prison, banging on doors, demanding to see his daughter. He had only calmed down when he was told I would be in court the following morning. Even that had been difficult: he saw for the first time the people I had been associating with.

'They are so scruffy,' he said with disdain. Well, they'd just come out of prison, I retorted. But you still manage to look neat, he said. It was true; I was wearing a denim pencil skirt and a close-fitting, waist-length cardigan. I had not yet adopted the uniform of my new tribe. This was the seventies and the style was long, floppy hair, for both men and women, and shapeless Indian cotton dresses and dangling bellbottoms.

My father believed in taking pride in one's appearance. His bearing, right until his death, was always proud and erect. His hair, thick and dark, was regularly trimmed and shaped. He insisted on his cotton shirts being perfectly ironed – one of the many things that put me off wifedom was the burden this put on my mother. She didn't iron the shirts herself but had to keep constant, anxious vigilance over Gladys, who did.

Over the years, as I became increasingly politically involved first as student leader and then as journalist, and people close to me were detained and tortured by the security police, my father remained supportive but anxious. I think it helped that he was inadvertently becoming an activist himself through his exposing the monopolistic, anti-poor nature of the apartheid economy and the pushback he encountered from the corporate world.

After university, I got a job on a newspaper. In one respect, my work was exhilarating. I felt I was at the cutting edge of a monumentally important struggle, exposing the evils of apartheid and giving voice to the liberation struggle. There was the comfort of certainty: it was literally black and white, and we were unequivocally on the black side. The forces of good against the forces of evil. And we were part of an intensely supportive community: 'the white left', we called ourselves. Yet we were small and beleaguered: our conviction that all other white people were on the wrong side was probably exaggerated. Nevertheless, we felt them to be hostile. Contact with black people, our natural community, was limited by apartheid's pervasive grip.

It was at the Quartalehouse in McGregor that I told my parents I intended to leave the country. I remember my father's face suddenly crumpling inwards and realising for the first time – with a pang of the old enemy, guilt – that while for me this step felt bold and exhilarating, for him and my mother it meant loss.

But I was desperate to get out of what felt like a stifling, claustrophobic world. Apartheid seemed invincible and increasingly oppressive. It was only later that it became apparent that these were its death throes. By then, I was ensconced in the *Guardian* newsroom, embarking on a new life.

I think that what I first fell in love with at *The Guardian* was its apparent lightness of spirit, which was intoxicating after the newsrooms I had come from. At home, late-stage apartheid newspapers, particularly liberal newspapers, were sites of war: pre-internet, they were one of the few channels from which people got information that was not controlled by a secretive, paranoid, repressive state.

I remember, night after night, right on deadline, reading my story out to a lawyer on the phone: not for libel or defamation, but for whether it could be contravening one of the hundred-odd laws governing which information was allowed to be printed or aired. And then having to frantically trim and edit. Security police bugged our phones and every newsroom had at least one journalist who doubled up as a government spy.

Every newsroom had a few journalists like me who saw themselves as conduits for the liberation movement: a vital channel for getting news out. I remember thinking guiltily once – and then quickly suppressing the thought – that the biggest danger for me morally was enjoying journalism for its own sake.

At *The Guardian*, where I started off as a subeditor on the arts desk, my world was opera and film, music and ballet. The arts desk was an island at the back of the features department: a sprawling, low-ceilinged room on the first floor of the old offices in Farringdon Road. The air was thick and muggy with cigarette smoke until the features editor, Alan Rusbridger – who later became editor – ordered a referendum. The non-smokers narrowly had it. The smokers were exiled to the lobby and we non-smokers no longer had to inhale their smoke. I loved this little show of democracy in action and the fact that it showed your vote counted, not something I was used to in my own country.

The highlight of the day was the twice-daily arrival of the tea trolley. Mid-morning and mid-afternoon, a canteen staffer would wheel in a trolley bearing coffee, a variety of teas, sweets and cakes. A representative from each desk – the features, the *Weekend Guardian*, the books desk, the obits desk – would take their colleagues' orders and join the queue where they'd idle away a few minutes in gossip, breaking the monotony of the day. In the evening, this was repeated at the grimy pub over the road: the Coach and Horses, with its wooden benches and jukebox, the tea and coffee replaced with wine and beer.

The hours were civilised and the holidays generous. And there were perks: the odd ticket to the Royal Opera House or the theatre.

Over time I discovered that beneath this benign exterior, politics writhed. From what I saw, it was class-based: northern, working-class men dominated the subs' desk and saw any fraternisation with the boss class as class treachery. There were 'gentlemen' and 'players': the former were the writers and editors, a substantial proportion of whom had been privately schooled and/or were Oxbridge graduates, and the subs, who fell into the latter category. I was liberated from this by my outsider status, feeling a pull in neither direction.

I worked hard and was promoted to deputy editor of the Comment and Analysis section: the three-page spread of opinion at the heart of the paper. Our reach was global, our aim to reflect and stimulate cutting-edge thinking on the big issues of the day.

I felt as if I were finally at the centre of the world, as far as I could possibly be from isolated, insular South

Africa. Every day my inbox was flooded with pithy, one-paragraph pitches from the great thinkers of the day, the powerful and the pushy, of which we could run only a fraction. The Labour Party, the political home of most of our readers, was in power and our opinion pages were influential. Everyone wanted to be on them.

On 9/11, the day the planes flew into the Twin Towers, I was having lunch at the Gay Hussar in Soho with a former leader of the Labour Party, Lord Roy Hattersley, who was one of our columnists. I dropped my spoon into my beetroot soup and hared back to Farringdon Road where I spent the next few hours frantically trying to commission piercing thinkpieces about a situation still opaque, a task further complicated by the fact that all international phone lines were down.

Stimulating as my job was, it was also exhausting. It started at 7 a.m. when I tuned into the *Today* programme on BBC Radio 4, which largely set the news agenda for the day, and seldom ended before 9 p.m., once all three pages had been put to bed.

And I never stopped missing home. When I first arrived in the UK, I found its low, clouded skies comforting after the relentless glare of South Africa's high blue skies. Now I longed for that sky's light, and South Africa's life-and-death intensity.

London dinner-party conversations revolved around house prices and where we were going for our next holiday. In our pages, we pondered the 'problems' of Africa and advised on solutions. In my core I felt I was a player, not a pontificator. I felt more and more strongly that I wanted to be out there, doing something about these problems.

I found British attitudes to Africa frustrating. It seemed to me that the national psyche required that it outsourced its caring, vulnerable side towards the continent. Africa was cast as uniformly needy, chaotic, childlike. The role of British imperialism in Africa's woes was never discussed. Instead, the UK regarded the continent as a charity case and delegated its responsibility – and the shaping of perceptions – to its aid agencies. To some extent, the Oxbridge elite that dominated the media also shaped policy on international aid and ran aid agencies such as Oxfam which, of course, relied on donations to survive. Together, they shaped a narrative that was frustratingly difficult to shift.

This dissonance rankled. It felt as if I were being further alienated from my roots.

And I missed my family.

When I first started talking about the possibility of returning, my London friends thought I was mad to even consider giving up my well-paid, prestigious job and my safe, comfortable life in a rich and stable country.

It was a visit from my father that clinched it for me. In June 2002, London was having a good summer, with day after day of convincing sunshine. I remember him being irritated: 'I thought I wouldn't have to wear this damn stuff here,' he said, smearing sunblock on his face.

He had recently had a melanoma dug out of his cheek and had to be careful.

He saw how paralysed I was by indecision. I was increasingly unhappy where I was, yet fearful of taking the big step, of giving up a life I had worked so hard to achieve.

'Come home,' he said. And suddenly it all seemed clear.

There was another factor that weighed heavily: my mother, aged 70, had recently been diagnosed with Alzheimer's. It was devastating news, particularly for my father. I felt I needed to be with the family: to spend time with my mother while she was still lucid, and to support my father.

Coincidentally, *The Guardian* had just started offering voluntary redundancies. I took the money and packed up my things. By Christmas 2002, I was back home.

That Christmas, over a festive southern hemisphere lunch of seafood and salads in a sunny Arniston garden, I chatted to Guy about Robert, our grandfather. Guy, the eldest grandchild, knew him best and he reminded me that Robert had, like his father, trained as an engine fitter. Unlike Alexander, Robert had lived in one place – Durban – all his adult life and had worked for the same company, BP, for 30 years, in a senior management role. Guy told me something I didn't know: that Robert had been given early retirement on the grounds of serious depression.

I wondered if his depression was rooted in the

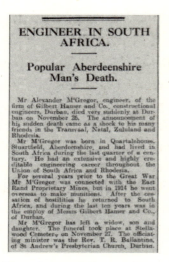

Alexander McGregor's obituary

hardships of his early life growing up as he had, with an absent father and an angry mother. He would have been an adolescent during the horrors of the First World War, which was swiftly followed by the Spanish flu epidemic. At the age of 18, he was uprooted from all that was familiar to make a life in a very different world with a father he barely knew. All of this must have taken its toll.

My father, too, spent most of his life trying to escape depression. Was it genetic, I wondered, or did he absorb it from his own father?

Nearly 15 years later, wandering the dark streets of Edinburgh, I thought of Alexander's trajectory: like me, backwards and forwards. He too had opted, finally, for South Africa.

Back in Cape Town, I find an email from a librarian in Aberdeen with whom I have been corresponding. In the archives of a local newspaper, she's unearthed an obituary of Alexander McGregor, published shortly after his death in 1929, at the age of 56. What catches my eye is the revelation that he had been 'connected with East Rand Proprietary Mines for several years' before returning to the UK in 1914 to make munitions.

I am intrigued by this because I know that ERPM had its own prison, the notorious Cinderella Prison, which supplied convict labour for its mines. Its most famous prisoner was the legendary Nongoloza, father of the Number gangs – the 26s, 27s and 28s – which, more than a century later, dominate not only the prisons but the criminal underworld more generally, particularly in the Western Cape.

The 28s have been implicated in my father's murder; I wonder whether Alexander brushed shoulders with Mzuzephi 'Nongoloza' Mathebula while they both worked at ERPM.

Perhaps it's just a distraction from the buzzing anxiety that has me in its grip, but I plunge myself now into history books, fascinated by this possible connection and eager to explore its context.

Like Nongoloza, Alexander was part of a period and place in history in which the shape of modern South Africa was forged. The British had finally vanquished the Boers and gained control of the Transvaal and, more importantly, its goldfields.

In June 1902, Lord Alfred Milner was sworn into office as Transvaal governor. His priority was to support the gold mining industry, disrupted by the Anglo-Boer War. Its restoration and renewed prosperity were crucial to his financial plans for the reconstruction of the Transvaal. Cheap black labour was also critical, and policies were set in place to ensure it was available.

In the cities, the movement of black people was restricted: they had to carry passes and mine workers lived in compounds. Under the Milner administration, failure to carry a pass became a criminal offence. Thus, ordinary working men could be jailed simply for leaving the mine compounds without a pass. As historian Charles van Onselen notes, the consequent criminalisation of the working class was to have profound consequences, not least because in prison the men were introduced to the Ninevites, the band of outlaws led by Nongoloza.

Much of what we know about Nongoloza comes from a statement he made to a Cinderella Prison warder in 1912. Born in 1867 in rural Natal, then occupied by the British who had defeated the amaZulu in a series of brutal wars, Nongoloza as a teenager found work as a groom on a white-owned farm. A horse went missing and the owner blamed Nongoloza, who protested vehemently that this was unjust – he'd been working in the garden at the time and the horses had been grazing freely. Nevertheless, the farmer, deaf to his protests, insisted that Nongoloza was responsible for the loss of the horse and decreed that, in recompense, the young man would have to work for two years without pay. The farmer threatened to have him jailed if he refused to do so.

Nongoloza was enraged and refused to accept this. He fled the farm and made his way to the nascent mining town of Johannesburg, where a chain of events led to the transformation of the naïve young country boy into the leader of a band of highway robbers living in the caves and disused mine shafts in the hills outside Johannesburg. They would descend from the hills to raid army pay wagons and camps. They also preyed on migrant workers on their way home from the mines with their pay packets.

He modelled his band on the ranks, insignia and uniforms of the Boer and British armies, which he subverted for his own ends. Nongoloza's army may have been thieves but they were thieves powered by an anti-colonial ideology.

Fired up by the injustice meted out by the white farmer, Nongoloza infused in his troops a sense of social justice. While their main occupation was robbery, they were also thought to exercise rough justice on behalf of the powerless, such as when a white employer failed to pay wages to black staff. Another hint of the ideological bent was in the name Nongoloza gave his band – the Ninevites, derived from the Old Testament book of Nahum that told of how 'the state of Nineveh had rebelled against the Lord and I selected the name for my gang as rebels against the Government's law', according to Nongoloza's statement.

Under the imprisoned Nongoloza's leadership, Cinderella became a Ninevite stronghold. Pass law offenders were mixed with hardened criminals, creating a black working class intimately involved with prison culture through the revolving door of mine compound and prison cell. In the next few years, Cinderella supplied a steady stream of new recruits to criminal gangs run by Nongoloza's lieutenants around Johannesburg.

I think of Nongoloza when I walk in the mountains around Cape Town. We are great hikers, Alan and I, and every weekend we explore the crags and crevices of Table Mountain. Glorious as these hikes are, I can never quite let go of an anxious alertness. Periodically, hikers are attacked by bandits and robbed of cellphones, wallets, cameras. Sometimes they are stabbed; occasionally there is a fatality. The advice is, never resist – do exactly as they ask. Give them what they want. Some of the bandits are gangsters, some just hungry and desperate. They disappear back into the mountains and are not always brought to justice.

I look again at the photograph I have of Alexander, proud paterfamilias, with the family with whom he had so recently been reunited, and realise that his lungs would already have been clogged with deadly mine dust. In the early days of mining, when Alexander worked at ERPM, safety precautions were virtually non-existent.

Any time spent underground would have exposed him to the fine silica particles in the clouds of dust constantly being thrown up by drilling. Most men who worked underground eventually fell victim to silicosis, some more than 10 years after leaving the mines.

Nongoloza, working above ground, would have escaped it. Not so my great-grandfather. Within a few years of the photograph having been taken, Alexander was dead.

8

Wouldn't hurt a fly

A new year, a new resolve. As January 2018 slides into February, I steel myself to start my exploration of Cecil Thomas's life, even though the very thought of it sets my nerves jangling, exacerbated by an ongoing insomnia.

I go back to my GP, who urges medication, explaining that the residual shock from the accident is bad for the brain and could have long-term consequences. I say I don't want the chemical cosh regime I was on after the murder, which was so difficult to wean myself off.

He suggests trazodone, an anti-depressant with a sedative effect, which will help me sleep. It has been in use for a long time and is considered to be safe. Reluctantly, I take the script to the pharmacy, feeling that this is a step backwards. But I also feel relief. I have again reached the point where I will swallow anything that promises to take the edge off.

The first hurdle I face is a practical one. I have no idea how to go about meeting with Cecil Thomas. A logical first port of call would seem to be the last place I had seen him: the Western Cape High Court. In its gloomy basement, I find a clerk who digs out the court records and transfers them to my flash drive. I go straight to a print shop and emerge with a thick wad of paper, several hundred pages long.

At home, I start reading – and discover that, shortly after the trial ended, Cecil Thomas's niece, whom I recall from the eloquent plea for leniency for her uncle, had written to the court requesting leave to appeal on his behalf. This was rejected by the judge who said his only doubt about the verdict and sentence was whether the sentence had been sufficiently severe.

Her letter includes a cellphone number. It is almost eight years since she wrote the letter and I have no idea whether the number still works. I stare at it on and off for several days before I enter it into my contacts list. And for several more before I summon up the courage to press the green button.

She answers. After I have identified myself, there is a long silence. Trying to sound as gentle as possible, I ask if we can meet. Anywhere, any time, I say, hoping I don't sound too desperate. By now the compulsion to get this thing done is overwhelming. Any obstacle would feel devastating. I am not angry, I say. I just want to understand.

She says she can see me on Saturday afternoon, which

is four days away. She will contact me before the time with a venue. By Friday night I have heard nothing, so I SMS her. She responds immediately, suggesting we meet at 5 p.m. the next day in the food court of a mall in the northern suburbs.

I get there early. The Saturday morning shopping rush has ended and the mall has a bleak, deserted feel. In the café only one table is occupied, by a couple with a small child. I choose a table as far from them as possible. And then move so that I am facing the entrance. I don't know if I will recognise her. The only image I have of her is in the witness box: a shapely young woman with long, brown hair, alight with love and grief as she implored the judge to show mercy.

The woman who arrives, dead on 5 p.m., is a little heavier-set but instantly recognisable.

'Liz?' she asks rhetorically, as I rise to greet her. It is a tremulous moment, for both of us.

The first question she asks is: 'How is your family doing?' This immediately brings the tears, which then set her off. We sit there together, two women weeping in a deserted café. I had not expected this simple humanity, this unguarded empathy.

My perception of her is informed by the man who links us, Cecil Thomas, who stands for the exact opposite – of dehumanised brutality. The image of him bending over my naked and bleeding father, slashing his neck, sticks with me. As do his lies in court and refusal to acknowledge what he has done.

What is also unexpected is how much Sarah (not her real name) and I have in common: like me, she is a middle-class professional working in the media. 'I was so shocked when you called,' she says tremulously. 'I never thought I would get a call from you. I was in tears for days.'

Her family, like ours, has been deeply affected by the murder. Half of them have cut Thomas off because of the shame he has brought on the family. 'Everyone looks at us as if we are murderers.'

What particularly upset her family is the fact that, unlike his elder siblings, he'd had opportunity: he had finished school and acquired a tertiary education.

'We are still in a lot of pain. But what can we do? We just have to work through it.'

Sarah too is haunted by the brutality of the murder. But she comes at it from a different perspective: 'I just can't see him doing that. That is not Cecil. That is not my uncle. He is a gentle man. Before this happened, I would have described him as someone who would not hurt a fly.' And then, softly, 'But you look at the facts ...' She tails off, shrugging.

The two of them are very close, she says. They speak frequently and she visits him in prison.

I explain that I want to look at his background to understand what brought him to that court. Cecil, she says, was not born in Saron but in Fraserburg in the Northern Cape Karoo, roughly four hundred and fifty kilometres northeast of Cape Town, where his grandfather had a job. Later, they moved south, to her grandmother's house in Saron, where Sarah herself lived. The family have deep roots in Saron, she says. Her great-grandmother had lived there.

Cecil is the youngest of 10 siblings. His eldest sister is her mother. Cecil is only a year older than her and they grew up in a small, somewhat isolated Saron community. As teenagers, though, they had been separated when she went to live with her mother in Cape Town.

Nevertheless, her granny's Saron home remains the heart of the family. Thomas's two children still live there with their mother, although she has 'moved on' and is no longer in a relationship with him. The separation from his children is very painful, for him and for them.

We talk about the trial, about how traumatic it has been for both our families.

I explain that, even after all the evidence, I felt I had only heard a series of stories. I did not know where the truth lay. Was her uncle just the fall guy, as he claimed? Were there others involved?

One of the problems, she says, was that the police and gangsters are hand in hand. Gangs pay off the police and then they run wild. The police are scared of them.

We hug as we part.

As I drive home, I think about the nature–nurture debate. Sarah grew up with Thomas: she must have had a similar environment and influences. Yet their outcomes could not have been more different. Now, as each approach middle age, Sarah is an engaged, responsible member of society: a wife and mother, with an interesting career. Thomas, meanwhile, is a tik-addicted murderer who has surrendered all his rights to a normal life. What was the point of divergence, I wonder, as I head back up the N1, Table Mountain looming large and comforting on the horizon.

That night, writing about the meeting in my diary, I note, 'A profoundly humanising experience: putting a face to The Other.'

I sleep well that night for the first time in ages. Partly because the meeting, although it lasted less than an hour, left me exhausted. But also because I feel a lightness: of relief, perhaps, that I am making some progress.

Looking back, it stands out as the most healing encounter in the long journey that followed.

The next day, I send her an SMS, thanking her.

My diary records our interaction: 'Got such a sweet note yesterday in response to my SMS: Still feel weepy when I think of it. Realise what a burden I have carried all these years. Feel a light undercurrent – of elation? Joy? Hope? Feel it might slither under the heaviness I have been feeling since the accident and sweep it up into the ether.'

Her note: 'I am so happy to hear that you feel much better. I am also very relieved. The meeting was really meant to be and I hope that you have a successful meeting with him too.'

My diary: 'I appreciated her courage and reliability and sanity. Now she will approach her mom and aunt and ask them to speak to me. And I know she will be true to her word.'

In fact, I never heard from her again.

But the information I got from Sarah helps me plan my next step. She told me that after sentencing in 2010, Thomas had been moved from Pollsmoor to Brandvlei Correctional Centre's maximum security unit, and after that to Voorberg Correctional Centre's medium security unit, where he is now. It was at the request of his mother that Thomas had been moved to Voorberg. It is just 20 kilometres from Saron.

I google Voorberg. It is about an hour and a half northwest of Cape Town. I find the contact details of the prison director and shoot off an email to him. The next day, his PA calls to say that I can see him on the following Friday at 9 a.m.

Alan is the only person I tell. He is worried: will I be safe? I must keep my phone switched on, he says, and call him with regular updates.

I leave home at 6 a.m. and follow the N1. Traffic is already building up in the opposite direction, heading into the city, but the outgoing lanes are empty. By the time the sun has risen, I have turned off onto the R44 towards Wellington. It is harvesting time in the vineyards and I find myself following convoys of trucks laden with grapes. Just after 7.30 a.m., I pass the entrance to Voorberg. I have a bad cold and am very anxious and badly in need of strong coffee and hot toast. I find it in Porterville, the next town, in a pub on the main road, which still reeks of smoke from the night before.

At 8.30 a.m. I pay my bill, do a U-turn and head back the way I came.

I turn into the Voorberg gate and onto a long, tarred drive flanked by tall trees. The first thing that strikes me is the majesty of the mountains into which I appear to be driving. Then I see the series of low-slung buildings crouching at their feet. Of course, I think. Voorberg. In front of the mountain.

Scrawny men in orange overalls pluck weeds from immaculate lawns. I am careful not to make eye contact.

At a guard post, a female guard asks me to open my boot. She makes a phone call to confirm my appointment and then directs me to a car park where I find a space under an awning. At the entrance, I sign in and deposit my cellphone in a wire cage. In the small reception area, I am asked to wait: the director's PA will fetch me.

She arrives promptly, a tall, elegant young woman who seems out of place in this fortress of delinquent maleness. As she leads me through a series of passages, she explains that every weekend she escapes to Cape Town.

The prison director, Bryn Wilson, turns out to be a tall, imposing man – a celebrated ex-rugby player, I later learn. His manner is businesslike. The only way I will be allowed to see Cecil Thomas is through their victim–offender programme. He fires up his computer and calls up Thomas's record, noting that he was sentenced to 30 years so will only be eligible for parole in 2025. 'It must have been a very brutal murder,' he mutters.

He punches a number into a phone and I hear him asking someone to come to his office. While we wait, he explains the history of the prison. It has the highest concentration of lifers in the Western Cape, he says. This is because it is the only medium security prison in the province.

Lifers serve their first five years in maximum security prisons and if they behave they are sent to a medium security prison to serve out the rest of their sentences. So this must have been Cecil Thomas's trajectory, I thought: his first five years in Brandvlei and now here because he behaved himself, whatever that means.

The director is still talking. Voorberg is a prison farm, as opposed to its apartheid-era incarnation as a farm prison, when prisoners supplied near-slave labour to surrounding white-owned farms. Now it is self-sufficient foodwise, with its own fruit and vegetable gardens and livestock herds. It has an abattoir and supplies meat to prisons all over the Western Cape. As he talks, I think how wholesome it seems: like some particularly successful, self-sufficient commune.

There is a knock on the door and a brown-uniformed warder enters. Wilson hands me over to him: 'Introduce her to the pastor and the psychologist. Don't take her to the correctional centre.'

'I will take her to my office,' says the warder.

To me, Wilson says, 'He will keep you safe.' It sounds more like warning than reassurance. As I get up to say goodbye, he repeats, 'You have to follow due process if you want to see him. You must be prepared. He must be prepared. The first meeting is likely to be traumatic.'

I could point out – but don't – that I am already traumatised. I just need to get this over with.

The warder leads me down a long corridor and through a gate, guarded by another warder, who unlocks it and then locks it again behind us. I follow him down more long corridors, winding snake-like for what seems like kilometres. We pass sturdy warders in brown uniforms and skinny prisoners in orange. They all look at me curiously, murmuring greetings. I assume that this is because a visitor is a rarity. Voorberg is, after all, is a long and expensive minibus taxi ride from Cape Town.

Once in his office, the warder also picks up a phone to summon someone. Pastor Zimri, he explains, the man in charge of the prison's victim–offender programme.

Zimri arrives promptly, a pleasant-faced man in his thirties. He shakes my hand warmly. 'This is a blessing,' he beams. 'A blessing.' They are very keen on restorative justice, he says, but usually they have to track down victims and ask them to take part. And here I just turn up on their doorstep.

Cecil Thomas may already have completed a restorative justice course, he says. If so, they can arrange a meeting immediately. Otherwise, they will need to prepare him first. He has to agree to take part and he has to acknowledge what he has done.

An image of Thomas in the courtroom flashes into my mind: he is looking at us directly for the first time and saying how sorry he is for what has happened to us. At no point does he say that he is in any way responsible for it.

But hey, eight years have passed, and he's had a lot of time to think.

Zimri asks, 'Did anyone phone you and ask you to do this? Did he phone you?'

No, I respond, it is entirely my initiative. It has taken a long time and much therapy to come to this decision. 'I'm very ready,' I say.

'What a blessing,' he marvels again. But Cecil Thomas must be ready too, he adds.

He says he will arrange a visit to my home in Cape Town with the psychologist to help prepare me and he asks for my address. I hesitate. He picks up on my reluctance. 'What is your nearest police station?' he asks. 'We can meet there.'

I tell him and give him my phone number, which he carefully writes down in his notebook: 'I will be in touch,' he promises.

Driving home to Cape Town feels like a long exhalation of breath. I have been into the lion's den and, hopefully, will get my reward. Soon, I will be able to confront Cecil Thomas. And then I can get on with my life.

I have inherited my father's Africana library, which includes a full set of South African genealogies, 24 weighty tomes produced by Stellenbosch University to record the family histories of 'the original immigrant families'.

I read that Thomas's progenitors arrived from various corners of the UK in the 19th century. Under numerous progeny spawned by a William Thomas of Herefordshire is a section subtitled 'Unlinked Persons'. Does this mean they became a coloured family, and therefore a subcategory?

Under 'Thomas' is a 'Charles Thomas c 1839', a bricklayer from Fraserburg. Charles Thomas had a son called Daniel Willem, also born in Fraserburg, in 1876. By 1894, this branch of the Thomas family can be found in Saron. Gideon Joseph Thomas married a Wilhelmina M Abrahamse in the Rynse Kerk (Rhenish Church), Saron.

I have no idea whether Cecil and Sarah are linked to this family but it is possible. Fraserburg, it turns out, is named after the Rev Colin Fraser, yet another Scottish immigrant to South Africa.

9

When the earth shook

Alan and I sit on the sunlit terrace at Twee Jonge Gezellen wine estate, sipping sparkling wine. It's a bit early to start drinking but this is the first time I have been back to Tulbagh since my father's murder and I can do with an anaesthetic. Thick white walls stop at waist height, giving a direct view of the vineyards climbing up the Ubiqua Mountains. On the other side of these mountains is Saron, home of Cecil Thomas. But I don't want to think about that now. I want to focus on the warmth of the sun on my back and Alan's arm draped across my thighs. 'This is the life,' I say, smiling at him, and we settle back into white couches so deep and inviting it seems rude not to stretch out for a nap.

The sommelier brings another bottle and offers us a refill: 'Night Nectar' reads the label. It is made from a mixture of chardonnay and pinot noir, he tells us. The farmworkers rise in the dead of night to pick the grapes when they are at their freshest, before the sun rises and steals their moisture. He pours the sparkling wine, palely golden in the sunlight, into our outstretched glasses. A fine-featured man in black T-shirt and jeans, he is flustered. We must excuse him, he says, he must quickly go and put on his uniform. He looks perfectly fine to us, but he is as disconcerted as if we had caught him naked.

A young couple come in, with a baby. They sit at a table near us and the baby hurtles across the honey-coloured tiles on all fours towards the fountain at the far edge of the patio. The woman, blonde and slight, in a sleeveless top, says something in German to the man and resignedly trails after the toddler. The sommelier rushes in, breathless, trussed up now in a jacket and ankle-length apron, dazzling white against the dark of his skin. The German man, alone at the table, gives his order, and the sommelier re-emerges a little later, balancing bottles, dodging the scurrying child.

I read out to Alan the description of Night Nectar on the tasting menu: 'Baked golden apples with jasmine in flower; notes of ginger and baking piecrust dotted with almonds evolves into lemon drops, sweet yellow apples and marzipan'.

Bloody hell. There's an entire bakery in here. We grin at each other. It is excessively delicious and I sip away, gratefully succumbing to the rising buzz.

My backpack is heavy with books and pamphlets I

have picked up from the tourism office. Lounging back on our cushions, I read bits out loud.

These mountains, I say, gesturing at the vine-covered hillside before us, are called the Ubiqua Mountains. 'Ubiqua' is another word for 'Khoisan', the original occupants of this area.

Then the colonialists in the form of the Dutch East India Company arrived from Europe and began a systematic clear-out of the indigenous Khoi and San so that they could take over the land. As more settlers arrived, the Dutch spread their reach inland.

In 1699, the governor of the Cape, Willem van der Stel, came to inspect the area and, I read out, 'was enchanted with it. In a letter to Holland he described it as a beautiful valley abounding with fresh streams, well wooded and eminently suited for agriculture. On Van der Stel's instructions, immediate arrangements were made for free burghers and immigrants from Holland, amongst whom were a number of Huguenot refugees, to be settled in this valley within the following year.' This very estate was one of 14 'granted' to Dutch settlers.

Within a few years, any remaining Khoi and San had been either wiped out or reduced to working on Dutch farms.

Alan grimaces. I gulp down more sparkling wine. 'It gets worse,' I say.

Tulbagh gets its name from a subsequent Dutch governor, Ryk Tulbagh. One of his major achievements, I note wryly, was the introduction of the Slave Code.

The Cape Colony was built on slave labour – the census return of 1754 showed that there were 5 510 colonists who, between them, owned 6 279 slaves. In that year, Tulbagh drew up the Slave Code.

I read it out: the preamble notes that 'notwithstanding the stringent proclamations that had from time to time been issued, the misconduct of the slaves was such that for the preservation of peace and good order it was necessary to collect all the laws into one ordinance, and to amplify them to meet existing circumstances'.

The second paragraph condemns to death without mercy any male or female slave who 'shall raise his or hand against master or mistress'. The 23rd condemns every slave found loitering about the entrance of a church when the congregation was leaving to be severely flogged by the ministers of justice. The 24th subjects to the same punishment any slave, adult or child, found within a churchyard at the time of a funeral. The 28th prohibits more than 20 slaves from following the corpse of a companion to its burial.

For many offences, slaves could be flogged at once by the officers of justice, without any trial. When convicted of ordinary crimes, they were punished more severely than freemen. Impalement, breaking the limbs on a wheel and slow strangulation were among the methods of execution.

The Code was pinned up at the Cape Town Castle, headquarters of the Dutch East India Company, in whose bowels were the jails and torture chambers where some of these punishments were carried out.

I suddenly notice that the German family behind us have become very quiet. Time for us to leave, I think. On our way out, we buy a couple of bottles of Night Nectar.

I have lured Alan here with the promise that we will do some serious wine tasting. I tell him that we can make a little holiday of it: it is, after all, a beautiful town, ringed by three spectacular mountain ranges with rows of orderly green vines marching down their slopes. It's harvest time and bunches of crimson grapes so ripe the juice is virtually bursting out of their skins adorn the vines like jewels, glinting in the sun. Several of the estates double as wedding venues and artful little white chapels spring up in the midst of the vineyards, offering a mistily romantic backdrop for wedding photographs.

He knows, though, that the real reason I want him to come with me is for support. I am hoping I can shed the horror I associate with Tulbagh and see instead what my father saw in it: why he chose to move here, where he knew no one. But it's an uphill struggle.

After we leave the wine estate, we take a drive along the roads ringing the town. I keep looking for a spot that might qualify as the 'beauty spot' outside Tulbagh where Cecil Thomas says he was taken by the gangsters to drink and smoke tik on the night of the murder. I look for lay-bys or any place where a car could have safely pulled off. It could have been anywhere along this view-rich road.

Back in town, we drive through narrow streets, dodging children and women carrying bulging plastic shopping bags from the Spar in town where Thomas met up with the gangsters.

Beyond the Victorian villas of the old colonial heart of Tulbagh is the 'coloured' suburb, with row upon row of small, boxy houses. These give way to a mass of shanties: rust-edged corrugated-iron sheets planted haphazardly on top of each other, each shack nudging the next. They seem impossibly flimsy shelters in this valley of intense heat and bone-chilling cold.

It is in these shacks that Tulbagh's most recent arrivals live: amaXhosa from the Eastern Cape, forbidden to live here during apartheid.

I have not been back to my father's house since the murder. Now, with Alan at my side, we head back into town and stop outside the house. Alan gets out to take photographs, but I stay in the car.

I remember him telling us at that last lunch at Groot Constantia about the woman who walked up and down this street, gazing at the house as I did now, after he had put word out that he was looking for a companion. His tone – light, amused – was one I heard from him increasingly often. After the long, dark period of my mother's illness, he had unearthed a forgotten emotion: optimism.

He was excited about this house and the new life he planned to live in it.

In his usual, practical, vigorous way, he wasted no

time in getting his comfort zone in order. With the renovations completed in record time, he had broadband and DStv installed so he could watch cricket and rugby to his heart's content, keep up with the news.

Shortly before my mother's death, he was diagnosed with a slow-growing testicular cancer. I thought this would have catapulted him into panic – he had always been a hypochondriac, or 'suffered from health anxiety', as my therapist taught me to say (I have inherited it). But he was remarkably sanguine about it, telling us with some glee that he was scheduled to have a new, progressive treatment that entailed having a radioactive pellet inserted into his testicle, which would kill off the malignant cells without damaging any surrounding organs.

'Sex will be off the table,' he said matter-of-factly. It didn't seem to bother him that much. It was companionship he was after.

He had always been on chummy terms with the local doctor – entirely free of the stereotypical male reluctance to seek medical care – so any potential problem was rapidly identified and treated. The depression that had long dogged him was controlled by medication, as was a tendency to high blood pressure and high cholesterol. He looked after himself, eating simply and healthily and keeping his weight in check.

Tulbagh was no different. We had driven past the doctor's surgery earlier, close to the house, and I recognised the name. Dad, characteristically, was already on first-name terms with him.

Other than the cancer, he was fit and healthy, as the post-mortem report testified, and his mind was sharp as a pin. On the day of the murder, he explained the subprime crisis then unfolding in the US to his young grandson in terms the child could understand, without sacrificing complexity.

His study was the largest room in the house. He still did quality control on the industrial sector reports published by Who Owns Whom. For light relief, he embarked on a series of books, exploring the various South African identities. He published them himself and I think it was largely for his own interest.

I note that the olive trees he planted around the perimeter have flourished, finally giving the house the privacy he planned for. But through the trees, I glimpse neglect. The grass looks brown and patchy. The jaunty yellow he had painted the house is faded and grubby. I am relieved when Alan gets back into the car, eager now to get away.

—

The next few days I spend in the UCT library.

I look for material on Saron. There isn't much. I know that it was established by German missionaries from the Rhenish Missionary Society (RMS) as a refuge for freed slaves, but that's about it.

Foraging through the library archives, I come across a book written in 1969 by Elfriede Strassberger, the daughter of two Rhenish missionaries, based on research she had done for her master's degree.

She records that the first four RMS missionaries arrived in Cape Town in 1829. 'On their arrival, they had thought that anyone could claim a piece of land for himself and gather heathens to teach and guide.'

They were rapidly disabused of this notion. The British had seized control of the Cape Colony in 1806, ousting the Dutch East India Company. It was essentially a slave colony, with slaves outnumbering freemen two to one. But this was soon to change and, with it, the fortunes of the German missionaries.

Leaving Cape Town, they travelled inland to Tulbagh, where a Dutch missionary had built a chapel and a school for the children of slaves.

Five years after their arrival, in 1834, slavery was officially abolished. But slaves had to continue to work for their masters for another four years as 'apprentices'. The owners received compensation for the loss of their slaves but the slaves themselves received nothing. As Strassberger records, for the missionaries, this yielded a rich harvest of vulnerable souls.

'On December 1, 1838,' she writes, 'the slaves were set free. This day proved to be of great importance for the work in the south. Erstwhile slaves came from every conceivable direction to live in the villages. Many had no homes and the existing houses were full to bursting capacity. Poverty and misery were found everywhere, as many were out of work. But the missionary was given opportunities which previously he had not dreamed of.'

The burgeoning number of recruits encouraged the Rhenish missionaries. In 1846, they bought a farm, on the other side of the Ubiqua Mountains, and divided it into 102 plots. Initially, 120 destitute families were settled there. They had to pay rent for their plots and they had to build their own houses. The plots were large enough to grow their own food and seasonal work was available on nearby farms. The missionaries named it Saron.

A church and a school were built, and by 1860 there were 1 000 residents.

However, the German missionaries frequently despaired of these souls they had gone to such trouble to save. 'The mission work at the Cape achieved financial independence with great difficulty,' writes Strassberger. 'The economic situation of the coloureds was very unfavourable. The missionaries complained increasingly about the excessive use of liquor, immorality and superficiality in their congregations.'

Slavery by its strictest definition might officially have been abolished in 1838, but its legacy lingered. The farm prisons scattered around the countryside provided cheap or free labour to white farmers. On the farms, men and women criminalised for infringing apartheid laws would have worked alongside the descendants of slaves, who themselves would carry the psychic wounds of a dreadful past.

For a snapshot of contemporary Saron, I look up

the results of a recent census. Most households have electricity, piped water and weekly refuse removal. However, almost two thirds of them receive either old-age pensions or childcare grants, which means they are very poor. Over 40 per cent of households are female-headed, which indicates a high proportion of single mothers. As in the missionary era, the only work available is on the surrounding white-owned farms and fruit-canning factories, which is largely seasonal.

Again, I make my way up the R44. Twenty kilometres before the turnoff to Voorberg Correctional Centre is a signpost for Saron. I feel I need to see the place where Cecil Thomas grew up.

I imagine him driving along this same road in my father's Mercedes-Benz, fresh from the murder, my father's blood on his clothes. I look for the cellphone towers which tracked his movements via my father's phone. On my right there is a large dam, with a man fishing from the edge. Sheep and cows graze on a field alongside it and a tiny foal trots behind two horses. This must be the dam in which he dumped one of the plundered safes and a gun.

At the entrance to the town is a large police station, caged in a high wire fence. Beyond that, a brightly coloured crèche, its front lawn generously equipped with slides and swings and roundabouts. A group of mothers, toddlers clustered around them, wait at the gates. It seems I have arrived at closing time and small children are tumbling out. I drive on and pass a library, a clinic and a large secondary school. Women sit chatting on the stoeps of the solid-looking houses that flank the side streets. Mothers push prams up the pavements. I don't see many men, nor does there appear to be much in the way of industry.

Like Voorberg, Saron and its surrounding farmland recede into a spectacular mountain range. A good place for a child to grow up, one would think.

As the town begins to tail off, I turn down a side road into what appears to be its dodgier end. Houses are small and shabby, interspersed with the odd spaza shop. A shifty-looking man, shrouded in a hoodie, is sitting on an upturned crate, a beer bottle in his hand. Mine is the only car in the road and I don't like the calculating way he is looking at me. I drive on and a black-windowed gangster car comes roaring up the other side of the road.

This is about as much as I can take of Saron. I head back to the R44, turning left at the T-junction towards Tulbagh.

This time, it's a research trip, another attempt to understand the town.

First, I need refuelling and time to reflect. At Paddagang, the restaurant in Church Street where the family gathered in the aftermath of the murder, I order coffee and cake. The waitress invites me to admire the resident owls, currently preening themselves in the vines looping through the trellis above us. It takes a while for me to spot them, their tawny plumage merging so seamlessly with the foliage. There are two of them: huge and wide-eyed. I drink my coffee, feeling observed, and go over my notes.

This is only my fourth visit to Tulbagh, each of which has been fleeting. I take out the tourist maps and study them again, hoping to see the town anew, as if coming at it for the first time, with my associations blotted out. But all I see is our country's painful history writ large.

I see Buitenkant Street, where my father's house is, which once marked the outer perimeter of the town. The main road is named after the predatory 17th century Dutch governor, Simon van der Stel. Parallel to that is Piet Retief Street, named in honour of the Huguenot descendant who led the Great Trek out of the Cape in protest against the emancipation of slaves and the increasing anglicisation of the colony under British rule.

Church Street, where I sit drinking my coffee, has been transformed into an elaborate memorial to another seismic event in the town's history. Literally. In 1969, Tulbagh, Saron and surrounding towns were hit by the biggest earthquake in South Africa's history.

The right of the map is blank. If the cartographer had filled that bit in, he would have had to include Helpmekaar with its painful, brutal history. It is Tulbagh's District Six. Like the iconic Cape Town site, Helpmekaar was a racially mixed, vibrant area, close to the heart of the town. Like District Six, Helpmekaar still stands empty more than half a century after it was cleared.

I pack my maps and laptop into my backpack, wave goodbye to the owls and step out onto Church Street, heading for the Earthquake Museum. It's a tranquil street, book-ended by mountains, huge oak trees providing welcome shade. It's not yet noon and already very hot.

Inside the museum, it is cool and dimly lit. It opens into an elegant room, arranged with furniture, artefacts and photographs, resurrecting images of colonial Tulbagh, pre-earthquake, and explaining how the buildings in Church Street were meticulously recreated in the original style.

Down a passage and to the left is another room. Here, at the back, tucked away, is the experience of the coloured people of Tulbagh. There are few artefacts and no elaborate architect's drawings. I assume this is an attempt at artful curatorship: a reminder of the deliberate marginalisation of coloured people. If so, it is much too subtle – almost apologetic.

There is a copy of the original 1966 Group Areas Act proclamation in the museum, announcing the new racial zoning: a neatly numbered and delineated town plan, with numbered erfs intersected by a neat grid of streets. There is a large rectangular area at the bottom right labelled 'Helpmekaar', outlined in blue. A key below it identifies the blue area as for whites only. This piece of legislation announced the apartheid government's intent to evict people of colour from Helpmekaar and give it to white people.

I ask the receptionist if there is a local historian I might talk to. 'My director!' she exclaims, happy to be able to come up so quickly with such a helpful answer. 'I will see if he is free.' I assume it is a white Afrikaans man who will be defensive so I'm thinking about how to frame my question in a tactful way when she leads me into an office and I see, with relief, an open-faced coloured man rising from his desk to greet me.

It quickly becomes clear that I have struck gold here: Calvin van Wijk is not only the foremost historian of the Rhenish Missionary Society in South Africa, but also has a deep personal knowledge of the area and its history.

'The earthquake was a very convenient excuse to move coloured people out of Tulbagh,' he says bluntly. 'Coloureds until the sixties and seventies were very religious, mostly Christians. Older people believed that you had to submit to the hand of God. The government represented God. They were told: "Can you not see that this is the hand of God? God has willed you to move and live among your own people." That is why they were so docile. They were told: your house is damaged. You must move. As soon as the houses were declared "unsafe", the bulldozers moved in. Racially mixed areas disappeared. They were declared white. Coloureds were moved from large-ish properties that they owned and sent far away to live in cramped social housing.'

Like District Six, the death sentence for this community occurred in 1966. It took 15 years for the apartheid government to eject the inhabitants of District Six and erase their houses. In Helpmekaar, the earthquake meant it could be done in three.

Feeling a need to be frank with this man who has been so open with me, I explain to him the reason for my interest in Tulbagh and Saron. He has not heard about the murder but he is able to give me valuable context on Saron and how what I have told him about Cecil Thomas's history might reflect the trajectory of the town itself.

The RMS controlled Saron for more than a century, only handing it over to the coloured arm of the Dutch Reformed Church in 1945, and Saron still bears its decisive stamp. The German missionaries dictated the architecture. Houses had to be built close to the street so that each had a large back garden where fruit and vegetables could be cultivated. The missionaries were paternalistic and ruled with a rod of iron. Literally, in some cases. There were strict rules and punishments for disobedience, which included beatings and banishment. Failure to pay monthly rental resulted in instant expulsion.

A community comprising former slaves who had known only their masters' homes, and Khoi and San made landless by colonial encroachment, they were desperate for a fixed abode. This made them very vulnerable.

The 1969 earthquake hit Saron hard. 'The earthquake was the undoing of Saron,' Calvin says emphatically.

'They were just as badly hit as Tulbagh but they didn't receive a brass farthing.'

Unlike Tulbagh, where government and donor money was poured into creating – and recreating – the ideal apartheid town, there was no help. 'People could not afford to replace their thatched or pitched roofs. To make things worse, they lost their free water. Under the *leiwater* [channelled water] system, they had been getting free water to water their gardens. After the earthquake, the water was diverted to Voëlvlei Dam. They had to pay for water and they couldn't afford it. This contributed greatly to the deterioration of Saron. The population became mainly old people and mothers with large families. They could not be strict with their children.'

The receptionist pops her head around the door to remind us that it is lunchtime and the museum is closing. Her face lights up when I thank her for sending me to Calvin. She is clearly proud of her boss.

On my way back to my car, I pop in at another of the earthquake relics: a Victorian house, perfectly preserved. A young Xhosa man proudly shows me a large, framed picture containing two dolls. They were made by the owner's wife, he tells me, adding excitedly, 'And, look, she used her own hair!' Thick, matte-blonde curls swathed around pale calico faces. It's weird, this fetishisation of the DNA of a long-dead Huguenot housewife. Every hair of the white head treasured, but darker, curlier ones spurned.

'Do you like living here?' I ask him. It seems to me unlikely: he is young and black in a slow-moving town where whiteness is the prized default and colouredness assumes the rest of the space. Does he live in one of the shanties? I wonder. If so, how does he manage to wash and dress in these clean, neat clothes in that space and be the face of a whitewashed Tulbagh, a rich tourist town?

But he answers immediately and with enthusiasm: 'Yes. Because it is safe. There is no crime here.'

I turn away. It is too violent a juxtaposition of my own experience of Tulbagh: a place of brutal death.

10

'The batons slip out of your hands when they are covered in blood'

Now that I have decided to meet Cecil Thomas, it becomes an obsession. It has to happen and it has to happen soon.

The courage I summoned to go to Voorberg and the optimism I felt at Pastor Zimri's enthusiastic response begins to dissipate as I wait for the phone to ring. Ten days after the visit, I phone the number he gave me. The person who answers says Zimri is not available. I ask for his email address and compose the following email:

> Dear Pastor Zimri,
> It was very good to meet you week before last. I feel as if I am in good hands for this journey towards some sort of closure. This is, as you can imagine, a very anxious time for me. It has taken me years to get to the point where I can engage in such a dialogue. I was wondering,

'The batons slip out of your hands when they are covered in blood'

first of all, whether there has been any news about whether Mr Cecil Thomas is ready or willing to take part?

Secondly, when I met with you, it was the first time I had heard about the Restorative Justice project. I would very much appreciate the opportunity to talk more to you about it.

Best,

Liz

No reply.

At about this time, I have a conversation with a friend, Patrick Giddy, whose 21-year-old son, Dominic, was stabbed to death in a street robbery. It is a sunny autumn morning and we are sitting in a corner of a coffee shop's lush garden, half-hidden by flower-decked bushes. I can hear the cooing of a dove and the chatter from a foursome of young women in gym clothes at a nearby table. Our conversation – about murder and retribution and overwhelming, inconceivable loss – feels at odds with this idyll.

Patrick's loss, though – if these things can be graded – is worse. In the loss of a child, he has lost the future. And no one has paid for it. The culprits were caught and tried but police bungling of the evidence led to an acquittal. This must have been devastating: to have to sit through a trial only to have the murderers get off scot-free.

But he surprises me. A clever, learned man, a former

Dominican friar who studied theology at Blackfriars, Oxford, and has a doctorate in philosophy, he has thought deeply about what outcome would have been most satisfying – or, rather, least wounding – for him.

'I don't want to see the guys in jail for years,' he says. 'What would be the point?' What he wants is a restitution process. 'I would like them to see the damage they have caused. And then tell me how they will make it up to me.'

Until this conversation, I haven't thought much about the philosophical or practical context in which I've sought my meeting with Cecil Thomas. For me, it is a raw, direct thing: I want to meet him so that he can tell me what happened in my father's house that fateful night. But I also want to confront my own fears – meeting him, I hope, will humanise him and thus diminish the monstrous dimensions he has assumed in my subconscious.

Later, Patrick sends me an extract from a paper he has written:

> I do see, as a participant in the social order, naturally, retribution, a restoration of order … my hurt, as a victim, pushes me to this. Still, there is another factor. The murderer remains in my, or our, shared community, walking the same streets, or behind bars in the same city. In my imagination, he symbolizes a block in my no-longer-open horizon.
>
> At the same time, the retributive feelings I have have

no necessary malice or ill-will towards the criminal. It is possible for me to find in myself a further appeal, to personal value.

This is where our society, as it is, continues to punish the victim. A process of restitution expressive of the deep human desire we all have, the victim meets the perpetrator, and this can ease them into a new set of healing images. Person faces person. Our inhumane society denies them this, expects them to deal with hurt by repression.

I'm excited by this because it echoes my own feelings so precisely. I open my laptop and google 'restorative justice', which leads me to a slew of articles and books. Briefly, restorative justice pits itself against conventional retributive justice. The theory is that the latter marginalises the victim and instead privileges professionals – judge, lawyers, police. The offender's deeds are seen as a crime against the laws of the state, and are therefore a matter between legal professionals and the state. The victim is merely collateral.

Restorative justice, on the other hand, foregrounds the victim and the offender. The idea is to facilitate a dialogue between them – and others who have been affected, such as family and even community – so that a common understanding of the crime can be reached. It helps the offender to understand how his or her actions have affected his victim and to take responsibility for the harm he or she has done. Together, victim and offender work out what the latter can do to make amends.

I read studies that show how restorative justice methods reduce recidivism among offenders and help reintegrate them into their communities. For victims, the process is particularly effective, reducing feelings of powerlessness and fear.

I think about how alienating the trial has been for us, my father's family; how incidental we and my father seemed to the process. How it only exacerbated our pain and bewilderment. Everything I read bolsters my determination to meet with Cecil Thomas. It feels like finally taking control of a process that, for years, has made me feel increasingly powerless.

Does it change how I feel about Cecil Thomas? Would I, like my friend, want him to find a way of making it up to me? I have a fleeting image of him working as a handyman at Ikhwezi, a preschool Guy and Liza run.

Ikhwezi is a project close to all our hearts. The other highway out of Cape Town, the N2, follows the Indian Ocean coastline all the way to Durban. As you leave the city, you pass Nyanga and the airport. An hour or so later, just after you have climbed Sir Lowry's Pass through the Hottentots Holland mountains, you see on your left a forest of shacks climbing ever higher up the mountain. Most belong to families who have come to the area to find work as seasonal fruit-pickers on the surrounding farms. Often there will be people at the

> 'The batons slip out of your hands when they are covered in blood'

side of the road, holding out R10 or R20 notes, trying to hitch a ride. In the middle of the shacks is Ikhwezi Educare.

It was started in 2006 in a small house on a plot donated to Ikhwezi by a priest at Guy and Liza's local Catholic church. It has since been extended to occupy neighbouring municipal land and offers a thorough preschool grounding to 150 children from very poor families. Two cooks make nutritious breakfasts and lunches for the children, often their only meals of the day. During the holidays, the school functions as a soup kitchen, dishing out thousands of meals to the community. Guy and Liza run this in their spare time.

Guy and Liza are the first members of my family I tell about my intention to visit the man who murdered my father. Both have a strong faith and are comfortable with the concept of redemption. They are, as I thought they would be, understanding and sympathetic. Guy, as my older brother, is always protective. I love him very much.

As quickly as I think of Cecil Thomas redeeming himself by working at Ikhwezi, I dismiss it. Knowing the brutality of which he is capable, I wouldn't let him near children.

One of the many things that keep me awake at night is the effect of my quest on my siblings. Initially, I kept quiet about it. I was barely staying afloat myself. I had no reserves with which to support my siblings through what would inevitably be a reawakening of the trauma.

The murder of our father was a profoundly destabilising event for all of us. Each of us has found different ways of dealing with it.

The journey I have embarked upon feels critical to my own healing but to my siblings it might appear a betrayal. We are a close family and I dread the prospect of causing them any further pain. I do eventually tell each of them, one by one. Once the shock has subsided, they accept it gracefully. If this is what I need to do to heal, they are at peace with it. I am profoundly grateful for this.

When asked how I feel about Cecil Thomas, I say I don't hate him or harbour anger towards him. Because I feel that would be corrosive. It would damage me, give him too much power over me. What I do feel is revulsion. And fear. Like Patrick, I experience him as a block on my horizon. In order to move forward, I need to break down that block. And to do that, I need to meet him, to understand him and thus demystify him.

Bryn Wilson, the director of Voorberg, said my meeting would need to follow the process dictated by the prison's victim–offender programme. So I search through prison legislation and in the 2005 *White Paper on Corrections in South Africa* find that a new direction had been determined, which focused on rehabilitation of offenders. This was to include education, skills training and the 'promotion of a restorative approach to justice to create a platform for the victim, the offender and the community, facilitating the healing process'.

The paper continues:

> The *White Paper on Corrections in South Africa* represents the final fundamental break with a past archaic penal system and ushers in a start to our second decade of freedom where prisons become correctional centres of rehabilitation and offenders are given new hope and encouragement to adopt a lifestyle that will result in a second chance towards becoming the ideal South African citizen.

Of course, it was Nelson Mandela himself who set the tone for this with the Truth and Reconciliation Commission, which sought to excavate the atrocities committed in the apartheid era, thus creating a common understanding of the past and paving the way for a just future.

Prisoners held a special place in his heart. I come across a much-quoted statement: 'It is said that no one truly knows a nation until one has been inside its jails. A nation should not be judged by how it treats its highest citizens, but its lowest ones.'

Still searching, I find a local NPO that claims to run restorative justice programmes in South African prisons. It is called Hope Prison Ministry and is run by someone called Reverend Jonathan Clayton. The website gives his contact details. I call him up and explain my situation. I ask if I can meet with him to gain a better understanding of how restorative justice programmes work within the prisons.

In my diary, I write:

I was impressed. He listened intently and responded decisively and appropriately. 'Two things,' he said. 'First, I will contact our coordinator and find out if Thomas was on the RJ session we ran three weeks ago at Voorberg or if he was on a previous one. Second, you must sit in on an RJ course – particularly on a Tuesday, when we run our joint victim–offender programme. The next one is at Malmesbury Prison, and I will send you the timetable.'

I am intrigued by this: entirely by accident, I have come across information that directly affects my quest. Zimri mentioned that he needed to find out whether Thomas had been on a restorative justice course before he could respond to me. My conversation with Clayton seems to reveal that it was he who would have run such a course, rather than the prison authorities. Later, I find that this was indeed the case.

I ask Clayton to hold off until I have a chance to consult Zimri and ensure that it won't interfere with any process he has already set in motion.

'Of course,' he replies. 'I won't do anything until I hear back from you.'

I call the number Zimri gave me. This time he answers and assures me he has no problem with my working with Clayton. He also says that, as yet, he has not had the time to check whether Thomas was on his restorative justice programme. My heart sinks a little. It is now two

> 'The batons slip out of your hands when they are covered in blood'

weeks since I have seen him – his warmth led me to expect that he was going to embrace this opportunity. Two weeks in which a prospective meeting has occupied every waking moment. How long would it have taken him to look it up? He seemed so delighted that I had turned up. Was it all just show?

I resolve to go full steam ahead with Clayton. Any action is better than sitting around waiting for a call that might never come.

I WhatsApp Clayton: 'Dear Rev Clayton, thank you for taking my call yesterday. I have now spoken to Pastor Zimri and all is fine. I would be grateful if I could meet with you as soon as possible. I am also very keen to attend the RJ programme at Malmesbury, as you suggested.'

I don't hear back from him but, nevertheless, it felt like a positive encounter. With the Malmesbury Correctional Centre visit on the horizon, I have at least got some momentum.

This is particularly comforting in light of the ongoing silence from Voorberg.

My diary on 4 April 2018 reads, 'Feel increasing frustration. It has been a month since my visit to Voorberg but I have not heard a word from them. I tried phoning Pastor Zimri again but he is not available.'

Meanwhile, I have a difficult decision to make.

I now have the dates for the Malmesbury restorative justice week and they clash with a hike I have been looking forward to for months. The Whale Trail, a

56-kilometre hike through De Hoop Nature Reserve on the Western Cape's south coast, is very popular and it could take a year to get another booking. I agonise for days over what to do and then decide to write to Clayton and ask him if there would be another opportunity were I to miss the Malmesbury session.

He replies promptly: there is another restorative justice session at Brandvlei Correctional Centre from 6 to 14 May. It is in the maximum security unit. The participants would be just starting long sentences for serious crimes. I could come to that instead. I immediately say yes.

Cecil Thomas was moved from Pollsmoor in Cape Town to Brandvlei near Worcester after the trial. He had served the first five years of his sentence there. Going to Brandvlei might help me understand his prison trajectory.

For five days, I do nothing but put one foot in front of the next, hour after hour. We start high in the mountains and make our way down to the sea. The weather on the southern Cape coast is reliably capricious. We are battered by gales; torpedoed by armies of horse flies; bathed in soft mists and bright, gentle sunlight. On the first day, as we make our way gingerly along a high, windy ridge, a flock of Cape vultures soar overhead, their wings so close and so vast we can feel the chill of their shadow.

Through gardens of fynbos, we trudge down to the coast. It is too early in the year for whales but we dip our feet in the freezing water and breathe in the salty air. We eat heartily each night and retire early to our bunk beds, so tired that sleep comes instantly and profoundly.

'The batons slip out of your hands when they are covered in blood'

We don't see another soul and I switch off my phone at the start of the hike so I can't access what little internet and cell connection is available. I am reminded anew of the spectacular beauty of the place I call home and the power of nature to silence the frantic, doom-laden inner voice, for a while at least.

Back in Cape Town, duly refreshed, I sit down at my laptop to start the preparation for my visit to Brandvlei. I come across several articles describing an outbreak of violence there in 2015, which led to the death of a prisoner. Several others were injured. Cecil Thomas was likely still to have been there then, so I read the articles with interest. One in particular catches my attention: a report on the evidence given to a subsequent commission of enquiry by a criminologist called Dr Liza Grobler.

Dr Grobler told the commission that, after interviewing the parties involved, she established that the violence was gang-related. Another prison was being renovated at the time and some prisoners were temporarily moved to Brandvlei. Gang members carry their gang history and ranking with them from prison to prison and one of the newcomers claimed to be a judge, a high-ranking position in gang hierarchy.

Brandvlei gangsters were suspicious of his claim and decreed that to prove his credentials he had to stab a warder. It was in the resulting melee that the prisoner was killed and several were injured.

Dr Grobler said that warders suffered post-traumatic stress disorder as a result, compounding the damage already done by previous incidents at the prison: one warder involved in the incident had been taken hostage twice; another had been stabbed with a homemade knife, and a third had witnessed a young prisoner being raped by an HIV-positive inmate.

What I find alarming about this report, given my impending visit to Brandvlei, is how ill-equipped warders appear to be to deal with prisoner violence. There is one particularly disturbing sentence in the report: warders asked that the batons they were issued with to subdue prisoners be replaced because they 'slip out of [your] hands when they are covered in blood'.

I find an email address for Liza Grobler and write, asking if I can come and see her. She replies immediately. She is currently on contract working in the parole system and is based at Goodwood Correctional Centre. She is happy to chat. We set up a meeting for 11.30 a.m. the following day.

Goodwood Prison is only 20 kilometres from the Cape Town CBD, just off the N1. Its proximity gives it a very different feel from Voorberg. In the busy parking lot, minibus taxis come and go, disgorging passengers and then waiting for seats to be filled up again. As I get out of the car, I see two young men taking it in turns to suck deeply on a makeshift cigarette. Weed? I wonder. A group of young women and small children hang around the doors to the prison. A tiny pink shoe lies on the pavement, lost or abandoned.

As arranged, I call Liza to tell her I have arrived and

she emerges promptly. A tall, slim, dark-haired woman, she greets me warmly, asking, 'Are you the writer–journalist Liz McGregor?' Not only has she googled me, she has also looked up Dad's case. In the 24 hours since I contacted her out of the blue, she has already done some homework. A good start: I don't feel that I have to start explaining myself from scratch, yet again.

She takes me into the officers' mess and gets me a cup of tea. I explain my mission. I expected an academic discursion on prison gangs from her. Instead, she is all action, asking for details. I weep as I describe the murder itself and tell her to ignore my tears. I know by now that I can't control my emotions with this bit, but that I will quickly recover.

When I tell her that it is now almost six weeks since I made the request to meet with Cecil Thomas, and that I've been waiting in vain for any feedback, she says briskly that this is not good enough and tells me that she will take it up with her boss, who is the area commissioner.

Meanwhile, she says, she can do a profile of Cecil Thomas for me, including his gang affiliations and progression. She can probably find Llewellyn Tobias, the gangster originally charged with Thomas, as well. 'He will be on our system.'

It is possible that Thomas is a 27, she says, 'Because they are the violent ones.' But there could also be a Bellville South connection and the 28s rule there. Gang systems in prisons are very dynamic, she says, and are interchangeable with street gangs.

Young men drift into gangs because it gives them a sense of power. In Brandvlei's maximum security unit, they get fully engaged. If, after the initial five years and with a record of good behaviour they are moved to a medium security prison, such as Voorberg, they face a choice. They either look outward and disengage from the gangs so that they can work towards a life outside and an early parole. Or they get deeper and deeper into the gang structure. We don't yet know which path Thomas has taken.

I tell her about my engagement with Jonathan Clayton. 'His programme is very powerful,' she says. But it is large-scale and there is lots of razzmatazz. There are other options, like the prison's victim–offender dialogue.

I would definitely prefer the latter, I say.

Like Bryn Wilson and Pastor Zimri, she says it is important that he admits to the crime. If he continues to weasel his way out of it, it will be incredibly traumatic for me. But, she says, it is still my choice whether to proceed.

I seize on this last statement. It confirms that I have some agency. What I understood from Wilson and Zimri was that, if Thomas refuses to admit guilt, I might not be allowed to see him.

As I leave, she says: 'You are very brave.'

I think it is kind of her but it doesn't make me feel good about myself or have any resonance at all, really. The compulsion is so strong that it feels as if I have no control over it. I just want it to happen. Now, already.

'The batons slip out of your hands when they are covered in blood'

In my diary, the next day, I write about my visit with Liza:

> The signs are good. I send her the court record, as she requested, and she immediately acknowledges receipt. The next morning, she sends me a WhatsApp saying that this is how she will communicate with me. She adds that her boss is on a course so she has been unable to speak to him but will do so as soon as he is back.
>
> Liza has been keeping me informed, for which I am extremely grateful. But it seems that she too is encountering roadblocks.

When I meet Cecil Thomas, I intend to challenge his version of events. So, while I wait, I pore again over the court record, looking for the inconsistencies in his evidence.

I have to force myself to keep reading the forensic evidence, fighting a wave of nausea. There are several sketches which illustrate, like some particularly violent graphic novel, how the attack unfolded. The grandfather clock lying on the floor in the hallway, the glass smashed. This was where my father was ambushed, as he emerged, naked, from his bath. The thick trail of blood along the passageway to the door of the bedroom. Here, the blood had spread into a pool. He must have been lying there, in great pain and bleeding profusely, while his assailant or assailants looked for the safes.

From there the blood trail shows how he was dragged

into the bathroom. His body, wedged against the bath, is shown from several angles. Rigor mortis had already set in by the time his body was discovered, some eight hours after his death, so his last moments are frozen: the right arm, crooked at the elbow, raised to his face. The right leg partly hooked over the gaping wound in his abdomen. Beside his neck is a large pool of blood, which must have spurted from his carotid artery.

The post-mortem report lists each wound, mostly stab wounds, numbered from 1 to 27. The size and location of each is meticulously recorded.

Number 4 is the fatal one: a 25 mm C-shaped penetrating incised wound on the right side of the neck. The wound tract goes through the skin and subcutaneous tissues and through the sternomastoid muscles and penetrates the right internal carotid artery. The direction of the wound tract is from right to left, and downward.

Number 17: multiple superficial scratches of different shapes and sizes. Most are well demarcated and linear.

Number 18 records 'fresh impression bruises on the posterior aspect of the left wrist joint'.

Number 25 shows he was punched on the right side of his face.

I search for clues. The bruise on his wrist would seem to indicate that one person held him while another punched and stabbed him. This would bear out Thomas's story that there was more than one person involved. The number of stab wounds might indicate which gang was involved.

'The batons slip out of your hands when they are covered in blood'

A forensic sweep of my father's car picked up blood stains on the accelerator and the brake pedal. But there was also blood on the passenger door and on the back seat. This was not explored in court. Thomas had admitted to smoking tik in the car and possibly he had done so in the back seat. But it was equally possible that the blood had been spread by fellow perpetrators.

By day, I obsess over these details, going over and over them in my mind. My nights are jagged and nightmare-ridden. It is the stealth of the attack that haunts me. How does one protect oneself against such deviousness?

My father had always been security conscious. Throughout my childhood, he had not only a locked cupboard full of rifles, but also a loaded revolver locked in the top drawer of his bedside table. In Tulbagh, the revolvers were in the safe in his bedroom. Every night before he went to bed, he set the house alarm. All this had been useless.

When I was a student, I did self-defence classes that showed you how to stab an attacker in the eye with a finger, ram the butt of your palm upwards into his nose, or knee him in the groin. This envisioned a man coming at you, fully visible, face to face – a semblance of a fair fight, at least. But what do you do with an assailant or assailants who secretly infiltrate your house, hide in it for hours, and only when you are at your most vulnerable – the alertness of the day giving way to imminent sleep – seize you from behind in a darkened passage and plunge a knife into you?

While you relax in the bath and perhaps daydream about your meeting with a potential new love, savour the day spent with your son and your grandchildren, all the while your nemesis is lurking in the shadows. Who then proceed to torture you for an hour or more as you slowly come to the realisation that this is it. The end of your life. You are going to die, now, in this house, no family at your side, no chance to say goodbye. With only your tormentors as witness.

Stabbing is an intimate act: you have to be close to your victim, able to feel his breath, see the terror in his eyes, feel the impact of the knife piercing flesh and muscle, see the blood spurting out.

As this scenario plays over and over in my mind, I have a conversation that further spooks me. I have dinner with an elderly friend who, after a stroke, has been forced to employ a full-time carer. Patricia, as I shall call her, cares for my friend with skill and compassion. She is physically strong, able to lift my friend's inert body with ease. At the same time, she manages the intimate tasks my friend is forced to abrogate to her with delicacy and sensitivity.

Patricia lives in a gang-ridden neighbourhood on the Cape Flats. Over the course of my friend's illness, I have learnt that Patricia's first marriage was to a gangster, and in getting rid of him, she had hoped to distance herself from the gangs. But, simply living where she did, that was impossible. Each time I visit, the conversation turns to the latest atrocity. Too often, they involve her own family. A nephew is shot in the face at point-blank range by another youngster speeding by on a motorbike, a helmet obscuring his face. On another occasion, she and her baby granddaughter are caught in the crossfire of a gang fight, the bullets flying past the baby's head, just missing her.

I listen to these stories with sympathy but also the same sense of impotence I felt at the Nyanga primary school. Can't the police do anything? I ask. She sniffs with disgust. The police are useless. They are in the pay of the gangs.

At that particular dinner with my friend, I tell her about my father and my quest to meet his killer. Patricia instantly seizes on it: this is deeply familiar territory. There is no way Thomas acted alone, she says. These guys always operate in a group. And there is no doubt he took part in the murder.

As soon as I mention Chris Langkop, she says, 'He is The Firm.' I must be very careful, she says. 'They know everything. They are hand in hand with the cops. And information goes from prison to prison. You are in danger if you try to reopen the case or take it further.'

I tell her about my visit to Voorberg and she shakes her head. 'The gangs will know who you are and why you were there.'

I feel my insides shrivel. Am I already a target? Suddenly I feel so unsafe. And, at the same time, I feel anger. What is the point of all this high-minded talk about restorative justice when the victim remains a victim? When the gangs are so powerful and the police so pointless? It seems that if you try to assert yourself against the perpetrator, you are further victimised.

In the early hours of the following morning, I wake up with an acid pain in the left side of my chest. I'm convinced I am having a heart attack. Then I look at Alan sleeping peacefully at my side and try to think rationally through my terror. Internalising the details of my father's murder has set those alarm bells in my traumatised brain shrieking again.

Nevertheless, I get up and lock the bedroom door. The police offered to return my father's gun to us after the trial but we asked for it to be destroyed. Now I regret it. I resolve to buy a heavy-duty pepper spray. At the same time, another voice is telling me that it's all pointless. If they want to get you, they will.

I lie awake until the dawn light peeps though a crack in the curtains. Alan stirs and I pour out my fears. He points out that Patricia said that I'd be in danger only if I tried to get the case reopened, which I had no intention of doing anyway. It's taken me years to recover from the initial court case. There is no way I want another one.

A week later, I have another night of hell. Patricia leaves a message saying she will soon have more information for me. She has arranged a meeting with someone who used to share a cell with Thomas. At the same time, she warns me, 'You put yourself in danger by pursuing this.'

I am immediately seized by the most desperate anxiety.

I try to call her back but there is no answer. She only gets back to me close on 9 p.m., by which time darkness has set in and I'm a gibbering wreck. Alan is in Europe and I feel a long night of fear stretching before me.

I beg her not to take any further action on my behalf. I don't want her to see this man. Do they know my name and where I live? I ask. Of course not, she says indignantly. I know how to go about these things.

I go around the house checking locks. And then – and it seems crazy to even me in retrospect – balancing chairs, ladders and pots against the windows, so that if someone breaks the glass, I will at least have a bit of notice.

I barricade myself in my bedroom, windows closed and door locked, the security company's emergency number on the screen of my phone. All night I lie awake, watching Netflix on my computer, listening to the foghorn down on the sea's edge, booming its message of looming danger.

As the darkness recedes, I open the curtains. Watching the heaving sea reflecting a shimmering pink back into the high, wide sky, my fears dissolve. There is a WhatsApp from Liza: No progress. Sorry.

I WhatsApp Clayton and tell him I will be at the Brandvlei restorative justice session in two weeks' time. Good, he says. These will be prisoners who are just starting their sentences. All have been convicted of serious crimes: mostly murder and rape.

Fuck, I think to myself. I veer between paralysing

fear and walking straight into the lion's den. What happens once this is all over? Once you have confronted this world head on, how do you retreat into a world of imagined safety?

When Alan returns, he says, 'You must find someone who can properly assess your risk.'

11

Can Liz stop?

It is at night that the Obz Café comes alive. Now, in the bleary mid-morning, it is half-empty, nursing a hangover. Towards the back, well away from the big plate-glass windows, stands Chris Malgas, an anomalous figure in his fatigues and with his erect, soldierly bearing.

We introduce ourselves and quickly get down to business. Sitting opposite him, still raw and jittery, I pour out my story. As usual, the tears come when I get into the detail of the murder. He doesn't say anything, just sits completely still, chin resting on steepled hands, gazing unblinking at me. It's slightly unnerving but I am left in no doubt that I have his undivided attention.

I ask the question that has been tormenting my nights, trying to make it sound businesslike because I am embarrassed by my feebleness: 'If I go ahead with this, will I be putting myself in danger? Is it stupid to put myself on the radar of Thomas and the vicious gangsters he is enmeshed with? Will I be looking over my shoulder for the rest of my life?'

He answers with a question, phrased in the respectful third person of formal Afrikaans, his eyes boring into mine: 'Can Liz not do it? Can Liz stop?'

For a moment, I am taken aback. I expected something measured, analytical. Some case studies, some statistics, perhaps, a weighing up of the pros and cons.

But then it comes to me how intuitive, how astute, his question is. He has instantly summed the situation up and given me the only appropriate response. Because of course I can't stop. I'm so fired up with adrenaline, so aquiver with nervous energy, that words of caution would have no effect.

All I need is the right person to hold my hand: someone with the right networks, knowledge and experience. But also with integrity and empathy. Someone I can trust. In that instant, I know I've found him.

Chris Malgas has just retired after 40 years as a warder at Pollsmoor, the biggest prison in the Western Cape and nerve centre of the Number prison gangs. Acknowledged as an expert in the ways of gangs, he works as a consultant, educating prison staff nationwide in their ways. Still deeply networked but no longer shackled by the inertia and politics of the prison bureaucracy, he can get things done. I am to pay him, but his fees are modest.

Out spills more of my angst. How shackled I feel by

racial shame. How burdened by our country's history, by the atrocities committed by people of my skin colour against those of Thomas's. How that knowledge undermines me and makes me question, in my darker moments, my right to hold Thomas to account.

Chris fixes me with a pull-yourself-together look and fires off more questions: 'Was Liz the architect of apartheid? Did Liz fight apartheid? Are you doing what you can to make things better now?'

I answer meekly: No and yes and yes.

'Stop the guilt and the shame then! Don't let your shadow block out the light! Your focus must be Daddy. Cecil Thomas not only took your father's life, he also harmed your family and brought fear into your lives. You have every right to call him out.'

Something changes in me with this conversation. It feels that, after weeks of grasping at straws, of batting feebly at half-closed doors, I finally have traction.

I tell him about my conversation with Patricia. I want to know how much weight to attach to it. His response is firm: 'She is trapped in that gangster world and must find ways to survive it. It was a mistake to talk to her. Don't talk to her again.'

I gaze past Chris to the street outside. A homeless man with shaggy dreadlocks framing a thin face knocks on the glass, trying to get the attention of a young woman typing intently on her laptop. In another lifetime, this was my hood.

I lived in Observatory for a few years in the pre-democracy era, first as a student and then as a young reporter. Still, then, mostly the domain of the white working class, rents were low and the Victorian terraced houses large enough to share with three or four friends. I remember earnest *Das Kapital* reading groups, furtive political meetings and security policemen hovering in unmarked cars. I remember a brief passionate love affair with a comrade, the different shades of our skin making it an illegal act, which only added to its intensity.

Now the remnants of the white working class have moved north and Observatory is more racially mixed than most inner-city areas. By Cape Town standards, property is relatively cheap and it is popular with emerging artists. And students.

Chris is not comfortable here. 'Where you get students, you get drugs,' he says bluntly. 'Where you get drugs, you get gangsters. Next time we meet in the southern suburbs.'

12

'I have traded my shackles for a glorious song'

The nights are longer now, with autumn deepening its grip. It is still dark at 6 a.m. and raining heavily when I arrive at Pollsmoor, where I have arranged to meet Chris. He may no longer work there but it appears it remains his centre of gravity. As I draw up, he emerges from the sentry box and hurries towards the car, hunched against the rain.

'And how is Liz?' he asks, settling into the passenger seat.

'Okay,' I say. Although in truth I'm bloody terrified. I feel a kind of liquidness, as if I'm lying half-submerged in a fast-flowing stream, hurtling head-first, eyes shut, to god knows where. I have no idea where the stream will take me but I feel fatalistic about it. I will land where I will land.

We are on our way to Brandvlei Correctional Centre

to witness Rev Clayton's restorative justice programme in action. I hesitated about whether to ask Chris to accompany me because I didn't want my experience of it to be filtered through his forceful, jaundiced gaze. But now I am relieved I did.

He directs me through the back roads of Muizenberg. Rush hour has begun and a steady queue of headlights comes at us from the opposite lane, heading into the city.

As we settle into the long drive through the Du Toitskloof Mountains, he fills me in on the subtext of the morning's meeting. Brandvlei is dominated by the 28s, he says. Only senior members of the gang will be allowed to speak. The leaders would have discussed it and decided whether it was worth taking part. This would depend on what they could get out of it. For instance, the final day of the programme is family reconciliation day and Hope Prison Ministry will arrange for their families to visit and pay for their transport. That means they can bring money. Perhaps even cellphones and drugs.

'Do you miss prison life?' I ask.

'I miss the people,' he says after a brief silence. 'I miss the charge of the work because every morning when I came to work, it was a new day, it was a new challenge. Yesterday is gone. There is nothing of yesterday. There it is dangerous, it is new; it is afresh. Because you work with human beings. I leave at 4 p.m. one day and when I get there at 3.15 a.m. the next morning, I find them different. They might have had a disturbing telephone call with people at home; or they are drugged; or they have come back from court. The case has been postponed. Or they have been found guilty. Or there is someone new.

'It's a high-adrenaline job. You feel it in your body. I can feel it now.'

But he is busier than ever in a consultant role. He still runs training courses on gangs for prison staff. He runs courses for convicted sex offenders out on parole. He helps people like me.

'By the grace of God, I have built strong rapport with key gang members,' he muses. But he must chart a delicate course: some see him as an infiltrator, who spills their secrets. He shakes his head: 'It was never my intention to infiltrate. It was more to understand the human being I worked with. What does he think? What emotion does he operate from? I wanted to view the world through his lens.'

There have been threats, he says. But his relationships have protected him. 'There is one guy in particular who was in jail for 22 years. I befriended him and we are very close. He will warn me sporadically: don't go there. Don't do this. Be careful of people coming up behind you. Many, many times.'

All his experience of prisons in the brutal, apartheid-era prison regime has reinforced in him the wisdom of treating prisoners with respect and empathy. If you treat them badly, he told me, you further brutalise them and they get angrier and angrier and, when they are finally released, they take that anger out on the vulnerable.

In 2004, he says, when tik emerged as a big problem in Pollsmoor, he was asked to work with the gangs. After that, he gained a reputation as a gang expert. He cackles loudly at this, self-deprecating: 'I'm not an expert!' He was given a new role, training prison staff countrywide in the culture, pathology and behaviour of gangs. I've learnt this about him now: that although much of his narrative is infused with passionate anger – against injustice and bureaucratic stupidity – it is leavened with cackles of irreverent humour. It makes him good company.

The turnoff to Rawsonville looms. I need Chris to direct me again now. He halts his reminisces and reverts to facilitator mode. 'How are you feeling?' he barks. 'Give me a feeling word!'

I think for a bit, peering through solid sheets of rain. It makes driving challenging but, at the same time, the drama of it after the panicked months of drought seems fitting and somehow comforting. 'Excited,' I say tentatively. And I find that it is true. After the long weeks of waiting, it finally feels as if something is happening.

This visit is part of the toughening-up process. Clayton has assured me that I can attend this session purely as an observer. I will be able to watch and listen, but there will be no pressure to take part.

As we emerge from Rawsonville, a two-bit town that takes about five seconds to drive though, a large body of water emerges, shimmering, alongside us. It is the Brandvlei Dam and the water swells against its banks.

Another hopeful sign. On our right, a rainbow arches, tiara-style, over regal mountains.

On we drive until we get to a gatehouse. A guard checks our ID books and searches our boot and then waves us in. We are now on prison premises, but it is another long drive along a smooth tar road before we reach the prison itself, backed into the mountains, as if at the end of the world.

Brandvlei's original purpose was to house convict labour to work on the surrounding farms. The present iteration is only a few years old. There is no shortage of space and the prison is divided into a sprawling complex of hexagonal buildings, linked by walkways. One side is open to the elements, covered only by a thick steel mesh.

We leave the car in a near-deserted car park and run through the rain to the entrance. I am frisked in a booth by a female warder and my bag is searched – I have been warned not to bring a cellphone – and then we are led through a series of interleading corridors that culminate in a large circular room. Even the smallest slit of a window is heavily barred.

I am very aware that the exit is far away and that I am trapped in a room with some of the most dangerous men in the country.

Chris leads me to a row of seats marked 'Observer' at the back of the room. A young man comes up to greet him. Chris, it turns out, has known him from the man's earlier incarceration in Pollsmoor and he asks him what he is in for now. Rape, the man replies. He goes back to his table at the front of the room and Chris leaves me to greet the brown-uniformed warders sitting at the back of the hall. He is comfortable here, which I find reassuring.

While I wait for him to return, I look around. There are several small tables, around each of which sit five men in orange overalls and one person who is clearly a civilian. The men in orange overalls are African or coloured. Most of the facilitators are white. One of them, a young woman sitting at a table in front of me, gets up and introduces herself. She is an American volunteer, here for a few weeks, most of this time spent around men like these.

Each table is covered with a demure white tablecloth with a plate of biscuits in the centre. The homely domesticity of the setting feels weird, a bizarre juxtaposition with the men inhabiting it. Most have inflicted awful damage on fellow human beings, newly convicted of rape or murder or both.

They will be facing up to the fact that for the foreseeable future their lives will be shaped and determined by this institution. Its physical isolation reflects their own separation from all that is familiar. To survive here, they will have to find some accommodation with the cult that effectively runs it: the 28s. Most will join, if they are not already members.

This would have been Cecil Thomas's experience when he arrived here in 2010, at the start of his 30-year sentence.

The room is freezing. Cold seeps up from the concrete floor through my fur-lined boots. I have a spare jacket in the car but, trapped as I am in this circular room at the end of the earth, the prospect of retrieving it feels like an impossibility.

I'm jittery as hell. Grateful again for Chris's muscular presence at my side.

Jonathan Clayton walks up to the front of the room and taps the microphone. He gives a brief recap of the previous day's session, which apparently focused on the pain of offenders, rather than that of their victims.

Clayton knows about prison: he was jailed himself in the late eighties, for fraud. Since then, he has reinvented himself as the high priest of redemption. His Hope Prison Ministry is largely American-funded and runs most of the restorative justice programmes in Western Cape prisons, plugging the yawning gap left by the state.

Although I have spoken to him on the phone, this is the first time I have seen him in the flesh. He is slim, of medium height, with dark skin and dark hair. He leads and shapes the session, like a priest or an impresario. His voice is slightly hoarse: deep and confident.

'Yesterday, we were told about two of you who were raped as children. How do you feel today?'

He looks pointedly at a man sitting at a table in the front, who stands up and says, 'It was painful. But now I know that if you tell people about it, they will understand.' He has to shout and then repeat himself because the microphone isn't working and the rain is hammering down on the high, pitched roof.

A screen has been erected on the stage, onto which is projected a photograph of a woman with flowing blonde locks, a microphone held to her lips. An assistant presses a button on a laptop and we hear the blonde woman's voice, singing. The sound is crackly and comes and goes, but it has a powerful effect nevertheless.

When it comes to the chorus, the men join in. The words are printed on the screen, next to the blonde woman, and sound wells up from the floor, almost drowning out her voice.

> I am free from the fear of tomorrow,
> I am free from the guilt of the past,
> I have traded my shackles for a glorious song,
> I am free, praise the Lord, free at last.

I look around and see that most prisoners are singing. To a man, they have that focused, inward look, lost somewhere inside themselves.

When the final notes tail off, Clayton announces that today will be devoted to victims.

A young woman in her twenties is led up to the front. Clayton introduces her as Melissa. Her coat is wrapped tightly around her, like armour. She tells how, at the age of 16 she was raped by a schoolteacher, and for a long time was afraid to tell anyone in case she was blamed. She speaks of the pain and 'brokenness' she felt, traumatised not only by the rape itself but also by the shame.

I find her very moving. Although the attack on her must have happened a decade before, her pain still feels palpable.

Clayton asks the rapists in the room to come to the front. Six men file up. Clayton asks them what they want to say to Melissa. The first reveals that he is in for both rape and murder. 'I did not accept that I did it,' he says. 'Now that I've listened to you, I am seeking forgiveness. But how can I do that when I took someone's life? And there were children! It has also affected my family. They don't want anything to do with me. Thank you for being so open so now I can be open.'

On the face of it, it's an astounding statement of repentance and burgeoning self-awareness. I find it difficult to assess the genuineness of it, though. It feels just a little too pat.

Another rapist steps forward, speaking in isiXhosa, which is translated into English: 'I am touched by your story. I was arrested for sexual abuse. When I committed the rape, I was drunk. Hearing your story, it makes me realise how my victim felt.'

A third says, 'It is now painful for me to recognise what I did to this girl. She was crying and asked me to stop but I continued. She told me she would tell her parents. When I came home from work, I realised she had told her parents.'

Chris, beside me, is muttering, 'He is standing too close. He touched her. You can't do that to a rape victim!'

The rapists return to their tables, accompanied by a hearty round of applause.

Suddenly there is a commotion. The men at the table in front of us leap up as one, lifting their table aloft. I feel a jerk of terror and clutch Chris's arm. Only when they carry the table to the back of the room do I understand that the roof above them has sprung a leak and water is trickling down onto their biscuits.

Clayton meanwhile is making another request: this time he wants men who have raped but never been caught to come forward. Only one offender steps up, but he wants to make it clear that he is a murderer but not a rapist. 'My name is David,' he says in isiXhosa. 'My crime is not rape but murder. On behalf of the men of South Africa, I want to say sorry.'

Melissa is praised and thanked and then she quickly leaves the room, as if she can't get out fast enough.

A tea break is announced. One of the rapists, a little, tattoo-ridden fellow, comes up to me and asks if I would like tea or coffee. 'Coffee, please,' I say. Feeling bolder now, I attempt to look straight at him as I was advised to do. But he is the one who looks away, demure and polite: '*Melk? Suiker? Hoeveel? A vol lepel?* (Milk? Sugar? How much? A full spoon?)'

When the coffee comes it is too sweet, which feels appropriate in this setting. There is something surreal about it – these murderers and rapists sitting around, sipping tea and nibbling biscuits.

About two thirds are African; the rest are coloured.

To the right of me sits a scholarly-looking African man, wearing glasses. Chris is off in the lobby, greeting the prisoners queuing up at the urn. He knows many of them from Pollsmoor. There is warmth in the greetings, a depth of history. I feel again that I have chosen the right guide: he understands prisons and their occupants, on either side of the locked cell gates.

As we take our seats for the next session, the young rapist who came by earlier passes by. Chris asks him, 'Why didn't you go up when Clayton called for rapists?'

He responds in a mutter: 'I didn't do it. I am appealing my conviction.'

Clearly his appearance at this session devoted to restorative justice is premature.

Clayton calls the room to attention and introduces two women and a man. They are middle-aged; heavyset, bundled up in scarves and cheap winter jackets. Clayton explains that they were injured in the Worcester bombing when members of the right-wing group the Wit Wolwe set off a bomb in a shopping centre on Christmas Eve of 1996, killing 4 and injuring 67.

After the emotional charge of the young rape victim, their testimony feels a little flat. They were random victims of crazed white supremacists whose target was anyone with a skin colour darker than their own. It lacks the intimacy of the one-on-one violence perpetrated by the men present. None of them can feasibly apologise on behalf of the perpetrator.

After they have retired to their seats, Clayton starts

railing at how the government is failing victims whose rights, he points out, are protected in the Constitution. He reels off these rights: 'One! The right to be treated with fairness and with respect for your dignity and privacy! Two! The right to receive information! Three! The right to protection! And, lastly, four! The right to compensation!'

'None of this happens!' he thunders. 'So victims won't come forward. They are still bitter, angry, fearful. Victims experience disempowerment. They fear for their safety. Their rights are still being violated!"

So, I'm not the only one, then. My experience has been difficult enough, but it presumably pales beside that of most victims, who can't afford therapy and armed security services. Or pay for the services of a Chris Malgas.

We are coming to a close now. The blonde lady pops up on the screen again and this time I sing along, tears welling up despite myself.

———

It is mid-afternoon by the time I drop Chris off at his home in the southern suburbs. The next step, he says, is to compile an offender profile of Cecil Thomas. This will give us an idea of what his state of mind is, as well as which factors have driven him to the point where he is now.

For this to happen, says Chris, he will need to arrange

a meeting with Thomas in Voorberg. I wonder how he will manage this, given the opacity of Voorberg. I still have not heard a word from them. But Chris seems confident he will be able to cut through any bureaucratic tape. And my experience of him so far has given me no reason to doubt him.

The following morning, there is a WhatsApp from Liza: 'We have speeded up the process. Chris will go to Voorberg to do a profile on Cecil Thomas next Wednesday.'

13

Quartalehouse in the Cape

To distract myself from the tension of waiting for Chris to report back, I decide to spend a few days in McGregor, the village at the end of the road, tucked into the mountains, where my parents lived for nearly a decade. I want to immerse myself in a place where they were happy and productive.

I have booked one of the self-catering cottages at The Old Mill, site of one of my father's whackier forays. It is a large stately house at the top of the town, with a capacious veranda overlooking the town. It was here that he started McGregor's first-ever restaurant, an irony for a man whose idea of a good meal was mashed potato and bangers. This was in the early eighties, when it was still a rough, Afrikaner-dominated farming town, decades before McGregor and neighbouring Robertson became the hip, foodie destinations they are now.

After checking in I walk down to the McGregor Museum, which is housed in a small room at the back of the information office. Opposite, the weekly farmers' market is in full flow. I have a quick look: there is fresh organic rocket, tomatoes and peppers, olives, almonds and olive oil. Loaves of sourdough are laid out beside pastries, cakes and locally made cheese. People queue with baskets and cloth bags, chatting and laughing. I will come back later, I think, and hope there is still something left to buy.

In the McGregor Museum hangs a large photograph of my father with the inscription 'Former Mayor of McGregor and publisher of "Who's Who in South Africa"'. They didn't quite get the title right – it should have been 'Who Owns Whom' – but the photograph of him is compelling: his hair falls in a thick black wave across his forehead. He is smiling and looking intently into the camera: a confident, optimistic, engaged man.

A file beneath the photograph contains a letter written by my mother to the founder of the museum, a friend of hers, who must have asked her to explain how the McGregors came to live in the town.

In her letter, entitled 'The McGregors buy in McGregor', my mother wrote:

> Our Christmas 1969 was to be a never-to-be-forgotten one. We left the sugar mill on the KwaZulu-Natal north coast, where Robin was Managing Director, packed into a Valiant station wagon. I say packed because there

were eight of us, Robin and I, Robin's Aunt Dolly and our five children and all our luggage. Aunt Dolly, whose maiden name was McGregor, suggested that, as we were going via Worcester, we should pop in at a village called McGregor situated at the foot of the Riviersonderend Mountains.

We duly crossed the beautiful Breede River after passing through an avenue of stately gum trees. After 20-odd kilometres of orderly vineyards and the rolling green pastures of a horse stud, we suddenly entered another age. Whitewashed cottages of Cape Dutch, Victorian and Georgian style intermingled with fields of apricot trees bordered by life-giving water-beurt [*leiwater*] slots. We decided to visit the Town Clerk and see whether there was a possibility of buying a small plot.

He showed us the Council Chamber next door where there were photographs of the austere gentleman and his wife after whom the village was named. He was the Rev Andrew McGregor and his wife, Elizabeth Ann. This was a remarkable coincidence as our middle son is Andrew and our oldest daughter is Elizabeth Ann. But a coincidence nevertheless as Robin's grandfather (and Aunt Dolly's brother) arrived in Durban at the turn of the century and had no connection with the Cape.

I walk down the ubiquitous Voortrekker Road, past a tree alive with chattering weaver birds, their yellow feathers glinting in the bright winter sun, to a large house on a corner at the lower end of the village. I knew it as Quartalehouse, the house where my parents lived and worked for most of the eighties. It is now a B&B, with a different name, and it is enclosed in white walls.

I stand outside, trying to remember it as it was then. It was a U-shaped house centred on a large terrace with a honey-coloured stone floor and a trellised roof, covered in vines. I remember many happy family lunches on that terrace, drinking wine, gazing at the Riviersonderend Mountains, sleek and mysterious in the distance. New partners, a couple of whom became permanent, were introduced to my parents on that terrace. The first grandchild had her first Christmas here.

The move to McGregor came at a turning point in my father's life. After restlessly wandering from one industry to another, he started a broiler business on a smallholding near Bellville. It soon went bust: he believed the reason was that he had been squeezed out by the big producers. This strengthened a growing conviction that free enterprise was a myth in apartheid South Africa.

He had first suspected this when he attempted to sell Glendale on behalf of the Paruk family. The only potential buyer who agreed as a condition of sale to keep both the mill and cane fields intact, thus ensuring no job losses, was Lonrho, the British multinational. Lonrho hoped to use Glendale as an entry point into the South African sugar industry. After the sale went through, Dad stayed on in his job and, on Lonrho's behalf, tried to find out who the major owners in the industry were. But he was stymied by the lack of published information.

He hated being a cog in a giant multinational and soon we were on the move again – this time to Pietermaritzburg, about eighty kilometres inland from Durban in Natal, where he got a job at Rainbow Chickens, one of the country's biggest chicken producers. After a couple of years, they dispatched him to the Cape to scout a base for expansion there. Once he had finished the job, they dispensed with him.

He decided it was time he became his own boss and started his own broiler business. He threw himself into it, heart and soul. The whole family was roped in. Dad was by now approaching fifty. This milestone seems to have given him a new impetus. It was less a mid-life crisis than a jolt. I don't think it was conscious; it was more a realisation that it was now or never. His children would soon be off his hands so he could take more risks and become the man he wanted to be, rather being someone else's man in a stifling corporate hierarchy.

Before I leave for McGregor, I meet Andrew for breakfast at the President Hotel in Bantry Bay. Andrew had a particularly intense relationship with Dad because they worked together for many years. We munch croissants and discuss him.

Andrew was 14 when Dad started the chicken business. He recalls driving trucks in the middle of the night to deliver chickens to the abattoir. 'I also got involved in handing out wages to the workers. I enjoyed all that immensely. I wanted to leave school and go full-time into the business. And I can tell you that Robin seriously considered it!' he laughs. (Andrew always refers to Dad by his name, because they were colleagues as well as father and son.) 'But Mom said no.'

He continues, 'Of course, that business went belly-up. I was too young to work out why. But I think the problem was that you had to feed those bloody chickens. It's like an airline with fuel. You have those relentless bills for feed coming in and if you don't generate enough cash, you can't pay them. We just ran out of cash.'

The collapse of Dad's first attempt at starting his own business was a blow. He lost everything and the family ended up living in a rented farmhouse in the middle of an Elgin apple orchard, not far from where Guy and Liza were later to establish Ikhwezi.

Dad had a new job, managing an apple-growers' co-op. Andrew and Simon were still at school in Bellville, where my parents had moved when they started the broiler business, so he rented a flat near the school and installed them there with Guy and a freezer full of pizza. 'Unbelievable, really, that they would do that.' We laugh, ruefully. Parenting was clearly no longer a priority for either of my parents.

We remember the farmhouse with nostalgia. It was large enough for all of us to gather there for weekends and holidays. We could pluck apples off the trees and swim in the dam. There was still a Mercedes in the garage. But Dad was bored and hated having a boss again. As he got into the new job, which included negotiating the purchase of millions of apple cartons, he was once again struck by the opacity of the industry, this time in paper conversion.

An idea began brewing. He went part-time at the co-op and began travelling around the country, spending hours in company anterooms, waiting patiently for reluctant company secretaries to give him access to share registers. This was pre-computers. Everything was on paper. He bought one share in every company on the Johannesburg Stock Exchange so that he could receive their annual reports. These were all laid out on the dining room table at the Elgin house to be scrutinised.

What he found was explosive, revealing for the first time that five conglomerates controlled more than 75 per cent of the Johannesburg Stock Exchange. When he was ready to go public with his findings he contacted publishers, but when he discovered that he would only get 10 per cent of the proceeds he decided to publish his work himself. This in itself was risky. He sold everything he owned – which wasn't all that much – and produced a fat hardcover book called *Who Owns Whom*. It became an instant bestseller.

It exposed the grotesque levels of inequality of the apartheid economy. As sanctions forced foreign companies to pull out of South Africa, the big local companies bought up the businesses the foreign companies left behind. It was all shrouded in secrecy, until Dad started adding up those shares on the dining room table in Elgin.

He resigned from his job and ended the lease on the

farmhouse. The family – and the business – needed a new base. He chose McGregor and created the house he called Quartalehouse, equipping one wing with IBM computers, which, in those days, were huge.

He suddenly became a celebrity. Journalists came to interview him, one dubbing Quartalehouse 'the electronic cottage'.

For my dad, information wasn't neutral. He was driven by increasing fury at the consequences of this concentration of wealth. The monopoly enjoyed by these behemoths kept prices artificially high and this hit the poorest the hardest. He raged about this whenever he was given a platform, which didn't make him popular in boardrooms.

But in 1994, when the first democratic government took power under Nelson Mandela, attitudes changed. He was invited to join the Competition Commission and was delighted at the power this gave him to block mergers and thus help introduce more competition.

'Robin was a courageous man,' says Andrew. 'He was terrified of public speaking, but he would get up on a stage and talk. You could see he hated every minute of it, but the audience loved him and that is how he became famous so quickly.'

Andrew and Simon, who had left school, moved to McGregor and began working with him. 'He taught me how to be an entrepreneur and that has stood me in good stead,' he says. But working with Dad was not easy: he was impulsive and easily bored, and not much of a team player. 'He was very smart, very creative and exceptionally good with numbers. He had a very nice side, but he also had that angry, demanding side. We had some serious clashes, but he always had the capacity to recover. He would back off and say I'm sorry. He didn't want to destroy relationships and he never held a grudge.

'*Who Owns Whom* was a brilliant creation. The book made a lot of money. The cash came pouring in. He couldn't print enough books. In those days, people used books. There was no other source of information.'

For the first time in his life, Dad had money to spare and was going to have fun spending it.

He launched a newspaper, the *Breede Valley Bulletin*, and established a print shop to print it. In Robertson, about twenty kilometres away, he opened the town's first-ever bookshop. The restaurant at the Mill opened only on weekends but from the beginning it was popular. The food was only ever average but it was washed down with plenty of cheap McGregor wine and it was a novelty, being the only restaurant in town. Commercially, as with my father's other quixotic ventures, it didn't even wash its face.

'I learnt from Robin to focus because he jumped all over the place. Once you start diversifying your resources and your energies, everything falls over. Which is exactly what happened,' Andrew says.

Within a couple of years, Dad had burnt through the profits of the book. Ever resourceful, he dug a phoenix out of the fire, managing to flog a 30 per cent stake in the Who Owns Whom company to Dun & Bradstreet, the global information giant, to tide himself over the next six months, which was as far ahead as he ever looked.

Andrew comments, 'He had that ability to be really creative under pressure and to rescue things. But we realised it wasn't feasible to keep running the business from McGregor.'

They moved, reluctantly on my father's part, to Johannesburg. They started an ancillary business, McGregor Research Services.

I was living in London by then, and a letter from Dad in March 1987 showed how they struggled. I had sent him a tape of Dolly Parton songs; Dad had a weakness for schmaltzy songs.

> Hi pet,
>
> You are an absolute star! Your taste impeccable! Or should I say my taste impeccable, as I don't see Dolly Parton as your cup of tea! Thanks, pet, very much for thinking of me.
>
> Unfortunately, we're having a rather tough time selling our subscriptions – in fact, only one sold so far – and Andrew and I are talking ourselves silly. It appears we should have done it the other way round – go out and ask them exactly what their requirements were and then put together a package that suits as many of them as possible.

I'm still confident MRS will survive but it's been quite a shock, as we really thought it would go like a bomb. Unfortunately, the money will be run out before we can change direction so we are having to fire staff. All in all, it's not a very happy situation.

Before we decide to stop the whole operation, we'll pare it down to the absolute minimum and keep battling. Thank goodness Andrew and Simon are both determined it should work, because they take a considerable weight off my shoulders.

Your job sounds as hectic as ever. You've got all the ability in the world so don't sell yourself short unless it suits you. But also take it easy and enjoy life!

Look after yourself,

Love,

Dad.

Andrew recalls, 'We started that business by the seat of our pants and we learnt by making mistakes. Every time you make a mistake, you pay a price. Most of my job was with the clients and there were always problems because we did things on the cheap. In those days, it was much more difficult to write software.'

For the last couple of decades, Who Owns Whom has been Andrew's business, and it has flourished, a highly respected source of detailed, original research on businesses throughout Africa. Until 2020 he continued to publish an annual hardcover version of *Who Owns Whom*, but the business is now entirely electronic.

'What I learnt from those early years was to under-promise and over-deliver. I got it right this time. As a result, our clients appreciate us. That is why we get 95 per cent renewals every year. I never ever get a client phoning to complain.'

We sit there over our coffees, Andrew and I, watching the morning sun glinting off the restless waves and reminiscing about our dad. About what a difficult, crazy bugger he was. But also, what a genius. And about how warm and generous he was. And how much he loved us.

—

In McGregor, I wander back up to the museum, looking for evidence of my father's time here. When he became mayor of McGregor, it was dominated by the Afrikaner farmers who flocked to the imposing Dutch Reformed Church in the centre of town each Sunday and, unlike anyone else in the village, received free water from an indulgent apartheid government. There were a few English-speakers, mostly arty, hippy types, attracted to McGregor by its beauty and tranquillity, hidden as it was within a circle of mountains, with only one road in and out.

Dad started buying up derelict cottages and restoring them. One of them was Sunflower, the cottage next to Quartalehouse, so named because it had a sunflower etched above the front door. This was to provide accommodation for visiting children. I see now that

Sunflower is outside the walls that enclose Quartalehouse. It must have been sold separately.

I have an ancient photograph of myself outside Sunflower, with three small children. I am wearing a dark-blue dress, which I made myself. My hair is held off my face in a messy ponytail. The children – two little boys and a girl – are grinning up into the camera, holding up hands painted bright yellow. The boys' skinny brown legs protrude from their shorts. All of us are barefoot. The smallest one leans against me, his yellowed hands clasped together. On a windowsill behind us are the wooden pole and curtain rings we had been painting a lurid yellow, to hang new curtains in Sunflower.

The children belong to Gerrit Davids, a local builder with whom my father partnered to restore the cottages he was buying up.

Later that day, I sit with Gerrit on a bench at the top of the village. It is on a small incline, with the reservoir and the Boesmanskloof in the Riviersonderend Mountains behind it. McGregor spreads out before us. The sky is bright blue and the sun has warmed the bench for us.

Gerrit wears an impeccably ironed long-sleeved shirt; a fedora is perched jauntily on his head. He tells me that he has had two heart attacks and has to take medication for high blood pressure and diabetes. His breathing is laboured, punctuated by chesty coughs.

He calls me Elizabeth, which he must have picked up from my father, the only other person routinely to call me by my full name. He refers to him as *'jou* daddy' (your daddy) and his memories of both him and my mother are joyful, wistful.

'You know, they didn't treat us like coloureds,' he says. 'Not like the others. Those were lekker days. We had such lekker parties. When a house was finished, your mom bought *pragtige* [lovely] cake and chops and wors and drink and we partied. We were wetting the roof, man!' This is followed by a chesty chuckle.

My mother, he reminds me, taught English at Langeberg High, the 'coloured' school in Robertson. 'They still remember her there, you know. She made time for them. She was so proud of them.'

This is true. I remember that. How she agonised over the children who came to school without having eaten. How she cherished those who showed promise.

My father had faith in him, Gerrit says, pushing him beyond what he thought he could achieve, sometimes hair-raisingly so.

In an attempt to stay faithful to the original design, the ceilings in the refurbished cottages had to be made from reed poles strung together. My father bought the reeds and string and delivered them to the house where Gerrit was working.

'I said to him, "I can't do reed work. I haven't the faintest idea." He says, "But of course you can do it. What's there you can't do?" I am thinking, I'm supposed to be doing this job and I know fuck-all about reed ceilings and I'm scared I'm going to land myself in the shit.

'But when I was done, *jou* daddy said, "This is fantastic, man! The string is much neater and tighter than that old stuff and the reeds are lying nice and straight!"'

One of the children who painted the curtain rods with me, Aubrey, has been in and out of prison. All traces of Gerrit's earlier exuberance disappear from his voice when he talks about Aubrey.

'I am beginning with land claims and we are talking about the history of the village. We had people from all over – from Namaqualand and Cape Town – talking about the history of the village. I was talking about how tough things were in those times. And when I started talking about how hard it was growing up, Aubrey got very angry. He said he is going to kill all those people.'

He gazes out over the mountains, lost in another world: as he speaks, the countryside takes on a different shape for me. The scene before me becomes a palimpsest of shifting images superimposed on each other as, in rapid Afrikaans, he creates a verbal map of his family's long habitation of this land. His great-grandmother was a slave from Indonesia, his grandmother's father a white man. He points to the mountain range opposite us: the village was tiny then, he says. 'That was where my family lived. In the mountains. We struggled growing up. My mother, it was toughest for her.

'The brown children were not allowed into school. They had to look after the animals. They were held back.'

Now he points down into the valley below us, to a spot in the middle of the village, the white, gentrified part. 'I was born there. In 1950,' he says. By then his mother had moved into the village. Their house was on a plot large enough to keep animals and cultivate fruit and vegetables. Animated, now, he says, 'It was a lekker time. We had cows and we sold the milk to the Nestlé factory. We grew apricots and they were fetched and taken to the canning factories.

'And then the land was taken away from us. Then the white people said the milk was too little and they weren't going to buy from us any more, only from the farmers. So, we sold our cows. The same with the vegetables that we planted. They had a trick. The dams were full of water – there was water for the gardens. Then they were so dishonest. They took the water away. So we couldn't garden any more. Some of us had dams with a windmill. They broke down the windmills and filled in the dams so that we couldn't store water any more.'

In 1972, Gerrit and his family were ordered to move from his house in Hof Street because it was now in a 'white area'.

'This is where I was born and grew up. What could you do? The police, the magistrates and the council came – what could you do? I was still young and tough: I said I'm not moving. The police said: you can't stay.

'We were very unhappy and angry but couldn't do anything. Apartheid was so heavy then. If a white man told you to do something, you did it.'

Along with all the other coloured people in the village, they were shifted to new housing, out of sight at the bottom of the village.

'The apricots stopped after we were moved. That was when they took away the gardens as well. We used to grow apricots and they were fetched and taken to the canning factories. But they then removed our water and gave it all to the farmers.'

Now, 76 allegedly ancestral owners of the farms and houses in white McGregor have banded together to reclaim what they believe to be theirs. Gerrit is one of them. He offers to show me the records he has to back up his claims, but this is not something I want to get into. I do not know how strong his claims are and what chances he has of success. What I do know is what I see: a man struggling with the present who is taking refuge in dreams of the past and of a richer, easier future.

As we get up to leave, he says, defiant and with just a hint of sheepishness, 'I have a claim on your daddy's house.' He looks at me, uncertain how I will take it.

I think for a moment of what my dad would say, and then respond. 'Good for you, Gerrit!'

14

Meeting at Martins

This time I offer Chris the choice of where to meet. He names Martins, a bakery-cum-coffee shop in Main Road, Diep River, deep in suburbia. I find a parking spot right outside. Glass doors open into a large, light room scattered with wooden tables and chairs. Most of the customers are white, middle class, middle-aged.

Loaves of freshly baked bread are piled on shelves. At the front is a table displaying an array of cakes. I walk past it and then double back to take a closer look. Dread about the coming meeting and what it might reveal has sapped me of energy. I should eat something, I think, and when the waitress approaches I point at a slice of lemon meringue pie.

I am early because I want to choose the right table: one in a quiet corner of the room, distanced from neighbouring tables. I plan to record Chris's findings on my iPhone and, given the content, I don't want eavesdroppers.

I settle on a table at the back, tucked into the passage leading to the toilets. My lemon meringue pie arrives with a cup of coffee. It is enormous and the sight of it makes me feel slightly ill. I push it to the edge of the table and drink the coffee. At 11 on the dot, Chris appears at the entrance and I rise from my hiding place and wave to him. He weaves his way through the tables, a brisk, vigorous figure, dressed in a tracksuit. He's just come from the gym, he explains.

The waitress appears and he asks for a glass of tap water with a slice of lemon. From his backpack he removes a notebook and places it on the table in front of him. He flips it open to the front page and looks at me.

'Is Liz ready?' he asks.

Ready as I'll ever be, I say, pushing the Record button. Chris has been to Voorberg to interview Cecil Thomas. This is the report-back.

The story that unfolds is this: Cecil grew up in his granny's house in Saron. As the youngest of 10 children, five of whom were girls much older than him, he was indulged. 'He was always the baby of the family.' The women of his family were particularly protective of him because he had a disability: a bad stammer, which led to him being bullied by other children.

He was close to his mother, but she worked in a factory that processed and canned the fruit grown on the neighbouring white-owned farms. It was largely his granny and his elder sisters who brought him up.

Into this maternal cocoon would intrude, every few months, his father, with whom he had a very different relationship. His father was a carpenter, a furniture-maker. There was no work in Saron so he travelled around the Western Cape, finding work where he could, and was away for months at a time. When he was home, he felt his job was to impose discipline, particularly on his youngest son. This involved corporal punishment and Cecil remarked bitterly that his father particularly liked to deliver these beatings in the chicken *hok* (coop).

The chicken *hok* was Cecil's domain. It was his job to feed the chickens and to clean the *hok*. When he forgot to do this his father would beat him, and leave him there, weeping. The *hok* was his 'safe place', so the violence that entered there with his father felt like an added violation.

When Cecil stammered, his father would hit him on the head as if his inability to express himself was wilful and could be beaten out of him.

Chris looks down at his notes and reads out a line: 'He said, My father picked on me. I could not satisfy him. I felt like I was the black sheep. I hated my father.'

In between visits, life was fairly comfortable: there was usually enough food on the table. Saron's rural setting, surrounded by mountains and fields, gave its children a freedom denied to most coloured children in the cities, crammed into flats on gang-ridden housing estates. Cecil remembers horse-riding with his friends and hunting birds with a catapult.

When he was 14, his father died.

A waitress interrupts: do we want anything else, she asks, looking at the slice of lemon lying limp and forlorn at the bottom of Chris's empty glass. No, thank you, says Chris the spartan. I ask for another coffee.

Chris looks up from his notes. Shall I go on? Yes, I say.

After the death of Cecil's father, everything changes. Freed from his father's restraint, erratic and flawed though it might have been, he looks elsewhere for male role models. Rugby becomes hugely important in his life. It turns out he has talent and his prowess on the field gives him a powerful confidence boost. Years of being undermined by his father and laughed at by other children because of his stutter have led to low self-esteem. On the rugby field, it is action that counts, not words. There, he can finally fully express himself.

He tackles and runs and scores tries and becomes a hero in a small community where a rugby player represents the zenith of masculinity. He becomes a hero to small boys and an object of desire for hot girls. After years of being marginalised, he finds himself a valued member of a tight group of alpha males.

I know the power of rugby, the ultimate team sport, to create bonds, from the months I followed rugby teams for my books. They see themselves as bands of brothers, bonds rendered iron-strong by blood spilled and bones broken defending the team and vanquishing the enemy. How often had I heard the vow – 'We will die for each other!' – often expressed most passionately after a fines meeting where numerous shots had been imbibed, ostensibly in the interests of team discipline.

Chris, a star rugby player himself at both club and provincial level, understands its lure only too well. From his experience as a prison warder, he understands its redemptive powers, particularly for troubled youngsters. Cecil was a good example.

'In rugby he found an avenue to express his masculinity. He could rise above his disability. But also, because rugby is regulated by rules, enforced by a referee, he could safely vent some of the anger and frustration that had built up over the years. It became an outlet. You can tackle, you can be rough, but there are certain limits that you cannot exceed. If you do, you will get a red card, a yellow card. You will be punished and the team will suffer.'

This newfound stature was intoxicating – perilously so. 'He has such a need to be recognised and the field becomes his stage. Because of the rugby, he is now big in Saron. He has influence. And he begins to overstep the boundaries. He feels he can challenge the rules. He begins to experiment with alcohol and drugs and to challenge authority.'

In 1993, a year after his father's death, another epiphany makes landfall in Thomas's hitherto cloistered life. It offers another, edgier, outlet for his rage, his burgeoning rebelliousness and his need for acceptance, to belong. It comes in the form of a movie he watches when he is 15. It is called *Blood In Blood Out* and it tells the story of a set of brothers in faraway Los Angeles who form a gang they call Vatos Locos.

Cecil and his closest friends – two sets of brothers – decide to form their own Vatos Locos. Eighteen years later, the letters 'VL' are still visible on his right upper arm. His first tattoo. His mother saw it and was angry and afraid. A tattoo hints at gangsterism.

Chris reels off the names of the members of the Saron branch of Vatos Locos. I start when I hear one of the names: Neil Prins. It was a Neil Prins whom Cecil Thomas phoned from my father's house to say, '*Ons het die kluise.*' The call had gone unanswered.

So Prins had stayed in Saron. Had he perhaps been involved in the renovations of my father's house? Was he the one who told Thomas about the money in the safes? Had the seeds of my father's demise been sown in Saron in 1993, with the formation of this gang? All this is racing through my mind.

Gangs need an enemy to define themselves and Saron's Vatos Locos found one in another Saron gang, the Bad Boys. Cecil Thomas said that the Bad Boys carried knives but the Vatos Locos didn't. Or so he claims, says Chris, his voice edged with scepticism.

If the rivalry between Vatos Locos and the Bad Boys wasn't violent then, remarks Chris, it certainly became so two years later. Cecil and his fellow Vatos Locos gangsters were at a local dance. 'While Thomas is inside dancing, a friend rushes in and tells him that Neil has been stabbed. Cecil goes outside to find Neil lying on the ground with a knife sticking out of his head. Cecil grabs a panga and chases Neil's attacker.'

In the meantime, someone has alerted the police. They catch the boy who knifed Neil and put him in the van. Thomas is arrested and thrown into the van too and immediately the two lay into each other.

'This shows me that by then he had no respect for authority,' Chris says. His membership of the gang made him feel invincible and his need to avenge his friend was his dominant impulse. 'The police then sprayed them with teargas and moved Cecil to the front.

'So that was the first time he was in conflict with the law. He was sentenced to two months, suspended, for possession of a dangerous weapon.'

This was to be Cecil Thomas's only conviction before that of my father's murder, which in itself is an unusual trajectory. Usually, murderers have a string of convictions, graduating in severity. What happened to Cecil Thomas between 1995 and 2008? Because even after this incident, he was looked after. Every opportunity was given to him to grow out of his teenage delinquency and become a responsible citizen.

After the knifing incident, Cecil's mother decided he was no longer safe in Saron.

He had passed Grade 10 and thus had a school-leaving certificate. This qualified him for further study at a technikon, as technical colleges were called at the time. Cecil applied to study boilermaking and welding at the technikon in Bellville and was accepted.

The family rallied round. This was a big moment for the Thomases. Cecil, the baby, would be the first to get the opportunity to study at tertiary level. It was arranged that he would stay with one of his elder sisters and her family in nearby Kraaifontein while he studied.

A new world was about to open up for the troubled youngster from Saron.

I notice that Chris has been glancing at his watch. We have been sitting at this table for almost two hours. He has another appointment.

I am drained, only too relieved to be able to put off the next instalment. I need time and space to assimilate all this, and gather the strength to deal with what is still to come. Chris has warned me it isn't good.

We arrange to meet in two days' time. Same time. Same place.

He leaves and I ask the waitress for the bill. She looks at the lemon meringue pie, sitting untouched. I ask her to wrap it. I give it to the car guard standing unsteadily behind my car in an attempt to distract him from trying to guide me out of an empty car lot.

The next day, I track down a copy of Taylor Hackford's *Blood In Blood Out* at Cape Town's last remaining DVD shop. The title reflects the cardinal rule of gangs everywhere: initiation into a gang requires the spilling of blood, and if you try to leave a gang it is your blood that will be spilled because it is likely that you will be killed.

That night, watching the chief protagonist, the swaggering, testosterone-driven Miklo, team up with his two cousins to form the original Vatos Locos in East Los Angeles in the early seventies, I can see what the appeal for the 15-year-old Cecil must have been. Miklo, still a teenager, has an abusive father and, like Thomas, is mixed race. Miklo's father is white and his mother Chicano. Miklo is not the only member of the gang who has father issues: one of his cousins has a fraught relationship with the stepfather with whom he lives.

The three of them – cocky, buff, macho, aggrieved – seal themselves into perpetual brotherhood with the letters 'VL' carved into their bodies. Like Thomas's Vatos Locos, they define themselves against a rival gang and, when a particularly violent clash ends in a death, Miklo is sent to San Quentin, the maximum security prison. Here, he claws his way up the ranks of a brutal Chicano prison gang.

Cecil Thomas would have seen his own pale brown skin reflected in that of the three cousins. He may also have recognised their sense of social dislocation. The year the film came out on the other side of the world was a time of profound upheaval in South Africa. Three years before, in another fertile valley a mere 85 kilometres away from Saron, Nelson Mandela had walked out of prison to lead South Africa out of apartheid.

The country was preparing for its first democratic election, due to be held the following year. It was becoming clear that, despite decades of humiliation and marginalisation at the hands of the ruling white party, most coloured people were nevertheless going to vote for them. This spoke to their own sense of in-betweenness – of being neither white enough for the whites nor black enough for the country's new rulers. In their insecurity, most chose to throw in their lot with the devil they knew.

Miklo faced the same dilemma in San Quentin. Gangs were divided along strictly racial lines: black, white and Chicano. When it came to forging alliances, Miklo tried to team his Chicanos up with the black gang to form a united front against the whites.

In Saron, remote as it was, this question of with whom to ally – the black party or the white one – must have been on people's minds.

15

Martins, Take 2

As usual, I am early, to secure my vantage point at the rear, with a clear view of the entrance. Chris, as usual, is dead on time, and quick to get down to business.

At the same narrow table at the back of the café, with the toilets behind us and the yeasty smell of baking bread wafting past, the next instalment unfolds. I am beginning to think of Chris as my Scheherazade, spinning out the tale of Cecil Thomas's descent into darkness. But it is me he is buying time for. Helping me to put off the moment when I finally come face to face with the man.

Today, he paints a picture of Thomas's arrival in the big city. How intoxicating it must have been for a boy who had known only the rural isolation of Saron.

Cape Town is a city of many parts. The fertile, sheltered suburbs that hug Table Mountain. The vast sprawl of the Cape Flats, where the black people who previously lived in these suburbs were dumped by the apartheid government. And then there are the northern suburbs, whites only under apartheid, which embrace Bellville and Kraaifontein, where Thomas now lives with his aunt.

The closing years of the 20th century, when Cecil arrived there, was a period of tremendous flux: apartheid laws that had governed people's lives for decades had been torn up. These included the Group Areas Act, which governed where people of different races could live. Suddenly people of colour were allowed to live in previously all-white areas – assuming they could afford to. Restaurants, bars and clubs were opened to all. So were universities and technical colleges, of which Bellville has more than its fair share.

'And students bring their own different dynamic,' says Chris. 'They are young, they have money, they have freedom.'

Where there are students, Chris says again, there are drugs. Where there are drugs, there are gangs. The Number gangs had spilled out of the prisons and onto the streets. Bellville was the turf of the 28s. A shadow economy had sprung up, channelling the sale of illicit drugs in bars and nightclubs, with the aid of protection rackets, enforced by the gang-controlled bouncer industry. Certain senior cops were paid off to ensure that the law turned a blind eye.

Students are ready prey. The big city, with all its glittering temptations, opens up a treasure trove of new experiences: alcohol, cigarettes and entry drugs like dagga. Cecil, the country boy from Saron, with no one looking over his shoulder, would have been dazzled by it.

Nevertheless, he completed his course, graduating with a certificate in boilermaking and welding. He found contract work in Cape Town. But Saron remained his family base. He had a long-term relationship with a Saron woman with whom he had two children, a boy and a girl. But there was no work in Saron and, like his father, he became a peripatetic artisan, earning money in the city and returning home when he could.

He continued to savour the delights of big-city life. Thomas said that it was at a dance hall in Bellville that he'd met Llewellyn Tobias. Tobias: the name leaps out at me. An image springs to mind of the sinister, diamond-earringed figure in the witness stand at the Western Cape High Court – angrily denying that he had ever met Thomas. Tobias, the self-confessed drug dealer, and proud member of the Terrible Josters and the 28s.

It was in 2006 that Cecil Thomas started smoking tik, beginning a spiralling descent into the vortex of addiction. At the same time, unknowingly, he was getting deeper and deeper into a different kind of darkness.

As we heard in court, Tobias's drug-dealing business was based in a flat above Mr Burger in Voortrekker Road, Bellville. Mr Burger – a cheery name associated with family outings and cholesterol-heavy comfort food – was owned by one of Cape Town's most powerful gang lords, Chris 'Langkop' Arendse. The flat, known as a *pellepos* (hangout), was run by Arendse's son, Ernest. Like the 19th century opium dens, customers were invited to smoke drugs here, as long as they were bought on the premises. In a welcoming, convivial atmosphere, free of scrutiny or judgement, they could lose themselves in the drug's heady magic.

Cecil Thomas was riding a wave that swept the Western Cape from the mid-2000s. Crystal methamphetamine was readily available and had become the illegal drug of choice. Known as 'tik' because of the ticking sound it makes when smoked, usually through a straw inserted into a lightbulb, it is very addictive, inducing a stratospheric high, which is followed by an equally intense low. The list of damaging side effects is long, and mounts with prolonged use. It includes restlessness, aggression and violent behaviour, anxiety and psychosis. But that comes later. Initially, under its spell, in the cosy atmosphere of the *pellepos*, Thomas would have been oblivious to its danger.

But it was a false sense of security. The people ostensibly serving him and watching over him were in fact looking for what they can get out of him. 'While he is in his trance, his watch and his cellphone will be stolen,' Chris says.

He drifts deeper and deeper into addiction, unaware of what he is getting himself into. 'Because he has no idea what these people are. How ruthless and seasoned and smart. They are not what they seem. They belong to something much bigger.

'He is getting his tik on tick, but the debt is growing. And then, at some point, they want to know how he is going to pay. Through his contacts in Saron, he knew about the newcomer in Tulbagh and he painted a picture for the gangsters. They listened as he described how in this house in Tulbagh – home of the *argitek in die geel huis* – there was silver and gold. The silver was the cash in the safe. The gold was the bronze of the Mercedes. And that is where they made the commitment to meet in Tulbagh.'

I feel a presence behind me and jerk my head around. It's an elderly man in a cardigan who has emerged from the toilets and is standing aside for another toilet-seeker coming from the opposite direction.

Chris notes my agitation. 'Are you all right? Do you want to take a break?'

'I'm fine,' I say. 'Go on.'

'He smoked tik before the murder to prepare himself, to suppress his humanity. He needed to be brutal.'

This was to be his transformation from juvenile to man: sealed in blood. My father's blood.

I know from the court record that while awaiting trial, Thomas was held in a small rural prison. Repeated attempts to get bail were refused. When a date for the trial was finally set, he was told he was going to be moved to Pollsmoor in Cape Town for easy access to the Western Cape High Court. He fought this strenuously. His Legal Aid lawyer took it to court, arguing that Thomas had been warned that he would be in danger if he went to Pollsmoor. 'Something would happen to him' while he was there, because 'he knew something he shouldn't'.

A century ago, Cinderella Prison was the nerve centre of the Ninevites, precursor to the Number gangs. Now it is Pollsmoor, in the leafy Cape Town suburb of Tokai.

The objection was overruled and Thomas was dispatched to Pollsmoor. It seems that while he was there, he finally realised what he was up against. His emotional journey is inscribed into his flesh. In the weeks before the trial, he acquired two new tattoos: on his left arm, below the old Vatos Locos tattoo, is inscribed the words 'When days are dark, friends are few'. On his right arm, another plaintive plea: 'Why me, Lord?'

'These are cries of self-pity and loneliness. He is saying that while he used to have lots of friends, now that he is in trouble, he has none,' Chris says.

Already partially groomed in the *pellepos*, Thomas now actively seeks admittance to the 28s gang. It is not a done deal. 'They do not normally take people with disabilities, and he still has this bad stammer.'

The 28s direct his performance in court and tell him who to give up. His naming Tobias would have been approved, possibly because he had already been fingered by Thomas on the night he was arrested – Thomas told the police that my father's Mercedes had been given to him to sell by a dark-skinned man with a limp. He told the police this man's name and where to find him, above Mr Burger. This move of his, directing attention to the drug den and, by implication, the gang lord who owned it, may have needed deflecting, in the form of the offering up of another sacrificial lamb.

Each night, when he went back to his Pollsmoor cell after a day in court, Thomas would have been coached in how to adjust his story to counter the evidence being presented by the state. I recall the judge's declaration that he could not remember when last he'd come across a witness who changed his story so glibly every time new evidence changed the existing story.

Two hours have passed. It is enough for one day. We arrange to meet the following week.

Chris is still trying, with Liza Grobler's help, to negotiate a meeting with Cecil Thomas.

I think back to where I was, where my father was, in 2006: the year Thomas was introduced to the *pellepos* that set my father's murder in motion.

An image springs to mind of dancing around a fire under a starry sky. It was at the game farm in the far northwest of the country where my parents were living. My father and I share a birthday and we had decided to celebrate it there.

That day, 2 August 2006, was a significant birthday for me, and most of the family and many of my friends drove up for the party. Those who couldn't fit into the farmhouse pitched tents in the woods near the waterhole.

After dinner, we danced around the big, round firepit under the oak trees. The region is dry at the best of times but by August there hadn't been a drop of rain for three months. It made for crisp, clear air and unclouded violet sky, punctured by a million stars.

It was to be the last of my and my father's birthdays at which my mother was present. The Aricept that had slowed the progression of her Alzheimer's for the past couple of years had ceased working and, in the rapid descent that followed, she had become almost mute and very restless. She would sit for a bit, alongside my father, and then she'd be up and off, striding around the garden, as if looking for something. Still slim and lithe, she reminded me of one of the springboks that roamed the farm. She would start and shy away when my friends tried to greet her. It was so disconcerting, this: the shell was there, like some sleight of hand – but inside was only blankness. My father kept her at the party for as long as possible but at about 9 p.m., sadly, resignedly, he led her away to bed.

Alzheimer's is a hideous disease: death by centimetres. A slow bereavement for us, her family. My father was inconsolable. She had been his mate for over fifty years and for most of that, I think, it was a passionate marriage.

Andrew and I visited retirement villages in and around Johannesburg. We found what we thought was the perfect one: it had cottages set inside their own large gardens as well as a frailcare centre that took dementia patients. We spent time in the wards, chatting to the staff and observing how they treated the people in their care. We left confident that our mother would be in excellent hands. Dad would have his independence in a cottage on the grounds but would be a short walk away from her.

He would have none of it. Instead, he bought this farm in North West province, at the arse-end of nowhere, surrounded by neo-Nazi farmers and drunk, downtrodden black workers.

We, his five children, watched with awe (and some exasperation) as, at the age of seventy-plus, he once more reinvented himself.

It was back to basics: he and his ailing mate against the world. He had guns, which he periodically fired off into the night – to let everyone around him know he was armed, he explained. He swapped his beloved Mercedes for a 4x4. With the help of an elderly and irascible but talented builder, he built a rather beautiful house for himself and my mother. He did much of it himself: the design; the electrics, the plumbing. He sunk a septic tank for sewage and put a tank up on the hill above the house for water. He erected a mast on a nearby hill, powered by solar energy, to give him cell coverage and internet access. Andrew made sure he retained enough of a connection to Who Owns Whom to fund this financially voracious adventure.

And in some ways, he did create a little paradise. Vervet monkeys clattered over the roof and baboons barked from a nearby ridge. He bought zebra, kudu and waterbuck and every evening he would take my mother on a game drive. When we visited, we had to have sundowners in the hide he had built overlooking a dam where the buck came to drink.

Yet he found no peace. My mother, now almost entirely silent, followed him wherever he went, her eyes fixed on his face. He changed her nappies, fed her, bathed her and medicated her, mostly for her incessant anxiety. She must, at some level, have realised what was happening to her, and it must have terrified her.

He hired a succession of carers but they invariably turned out to be dishonest or inept. No one of quality would stay for any length of time in such a remote place. Or he or my mother didn't like them, which happened quite a lot. I think neither of them really wanted a third party in the house.

The most consistent help he had was from Julia, the tiny, childlike local woman who came in to clean. Julia slowly drank her way through all the alcohol in the house. She had four children by four different men and lived with HIV, which meant my father had the added burden of taking her into town for regular visits to doctors and clinics. But she was a gentle creature and my mother would allow her to bathe and feed her, which gave Dad a break.

It's a truism to say that parents are always a part of their children and children of their parents. It's not just the DNA they share – the way they reflect each other in appearance, in their susceptibility to high blood pressure or cancer or brains or athleticism – but also the way their voices are lodged in each other's heads, part of the incessant, internal voice that shapes and directs our interaction with the world.

I've always been close to my father: I was born on his birthday, his first daughter. We are similar in temperament. I have always relied on his lucid, razor-sharp mind to help me think through any issue that was troubling me. The pride and delight he took in me – for him, almost anything I did was quite startling in its brilliance – has warmed and bolstered me throughout my life. Which is not to say that it wasn't a complex relationship, with its fair share of monumental rows over the years.

During those last years of my mother's life, I felt I lost him as a father. Every time I saw 'Dad' flash up on my cellphone, I braced myself for an onslaught of anger and neediness. He had deliberately isolated himself, yet he craved our company. My sister and sister-in-law and I took it in turns to spend a week or two at the farm, helping him with my mother. It was never enough: he was still alone with her most of the time and every few months there was some new crisis.

So it was no surprise to get an email from him early one morning in late July to say that my mother had fallen in the night and broken her hip. By the time he got back to his computer to write to us, she had already been operated on, apparently successfully.

At another joint birthday celebration, on 2 August 2007, exactly a year after that party on the farm, Dad came into town and we went to dinner at his favourite restaurant, The Grillhouse in Rosebank. With my mother safely recuperating in hospital, it seemed an ideal time for him to take a short break.

I told him I would come back to the farm with him and help him settle my mother back in once she had been discharged. But, as it turned out, she never left the hospital.

Exactly a week after that dinner, on 9 August, she died.

16

Martins, Take 3

At our next meeting, Chris delivers the bad news. Cecil Thomas is clinging to the story he told in court. He still claims he has never even been inside my father's house. Chris pauses, looking at me intently. 'It will be very traumatic for Liz to meet him if he won't tell you the truth.' He hesitates. 'I won't go ahead if I don't think you are ready to face this.'

I let it hang there, this sentence. But only because I want Chris to believe I am taking it seriously. The truth is that I don't care what Cecil Thomas is saying. All I want is the chance to confront him. I hold my breath, so fearful now that this is the end. That, again, he holds my fate in his hands. That his refusal to tell the truth will give him the power to refuse to see me.

'I'm ready, Chris,' I say urgently. 'I promise I'm ready.' He nods.

But has he agreed to talk to me?

'Yes,' he says. 'He will meet with you.'

And what a fucking relief that is. I feel the breath go out of me with the relief of it. Finally.

And so, the endgame approaches.

My Scheherazade has a final instalment for me. The picture he paints today is of Thomas's life in Voorberg.

'*Agter die berge*' ('behind the mountains') is the phrase prison gangsters use for solitary confinement. It is probably just a coincidence that the prison in which Cecil Thomas has ended up is called Voorberg – 'in front of the mountains', implying an openness, a vista. Because here, where the lifers – the murderers and rapists, in other words, the worst of the Western Cape's violent criminals – serve their sentences, a community of sorts emerges, centred on the gangs. In the case of Voorberg, it is the 28s who create the rules around which the community coagulates.

First, while awaiting trial and then in the maximum security unit of the Brandvlei Correctional Centre, Thomas's identity will have been progressively dismantled, as systematically and completely as in the most extreme religious cult. He is given a new name and a new family to whom he owes exclusive allegiance. There is a new code to live by and a new language to learn. Even his sexual self is colonised. 'They break you so that Cecil Thomas is Cecil Thomas no longer. He is Patat, a private in the silver line.'

A new recruit enters the 28s through two different

lines: the left or silver line, or the right or gold line. Initiation is either through sex or through taking blood.

'He is a private, which means he enters the line of 28 from the left side. The left side is your weakest side. When you enter from the right, you are manly, strong – a fighter,' explains Chris. 'When silver, you are weaker, you don't have the heart to do the stabbing so you will do the light, feminine work. I will be 24/7 ready to have sex with you. He is a wife, a *wyfie*. To be a *wyfie*, you need to be "British". Being British means they have to be dressed up in their gear.'

This gear means being dressed entirely in white, with a flower on the buckle and on the front of a white beret. In this case, it is entirely imaginary.

Being 'Britished' takes on a more concrete form when gang members are going to war. 'This is when they expect to get into a fight, either with warders or with each other. Even in the middle of summer, they will put on all their clothes and a towel around their necks. They ask you in advance for newspapers and magazines and they use this for padding, for armour. They often shave their hair till they are bald, so that if they get hit on the head by staff or in the fight, the cut is clean and doesn't become septic.

'Afterwards, you hear them say, "We fought under the British flag." I think this goes back to the wars against the Xhosa and the Zulus and the Boer War. They see the British as good fighters.'

Thomas will have had to learn to *sabela*. '*Sabela*' is

the isiZulu word for 'respond'. This means that if challenged by another 28, the recruit must be able to cite the gang's history, creed and rules. '*Sabela*' is also the name given to the polyglot tongue – a mixture of isiZulu, isiXhosa, English and Afrikaans – that is the secret language of the gangs.

He will also need to know the '*huis toe kom*' (homecoming). This comes directly from Po Mabasa who was, as legend has it, the man who set Nongoloza on his path, luring him into his cave and teaching him his ways. Chris's version is this: 'If you ask me, I say I am Chris Malgas from Mossel Bay. I need to find work. I am not particular as to what kind of work. So then Po Mabaso responds, Where you are going to, there is work but the work there is hard and dangerous. Many people die there or get hurt. But it is for you to decide whether you want to go there. But I've been there so I know. Rather come with me, Po Mabaso. I will see to your needs. I will see that you are safe.

'So when I arrive in the cave of Po Mabaso, I see there is everything I need. There are guns, there is food, there is dagga. There is tobacco. They steal the wages from passing migrant workers and they break into white houses and bring the goods back to the caves.'

There is no need to do the dangerous, poorly paid work on the mines to get gold. You can steal it from the white man instead.

Chris pauses for a moment and then adds, shaking his head, 'Voorberg is one of the most dangerous prisons in the Cape because it is run by the 28s gang on the mythology of Po Mabaso.'

Once in the Number gangs, the divisions of the outside world like race, culture and language don't matter. Coloured, African and white start off on an equal footing. Language, in our land of 11 different official languages – most of which are spoken by a small fraction of people, adding to misconceptions and general ignorance about each other – is no barrier in prison. Even the warders don't understand *sabela*: 'Two of them are sitting there planning to stab us and we smile at them because we don't understand what they are saying!' remarks Chris.

So, in the 28s, Cecil Thomas has found the sense of belonging he has always sought. He is in a position of privilege in that he has been accepted into the most powerful gang. His master protects him and supplies him with what he needs, including tik.

So, although his stutter and his reluctance to shed blood in the interests of the gang – stabbing warders, disloyal gangsters or any other victim at whom the gang points its collective finger – diminish his standing, there are other advantages he can offer. He has acceded to a position akin to slavery, providing sex on demand and doing any menial domestic chores assigned to him, such as washing clothes and cleaning the cell.

He also brings a skill that can be exploited by the gang. Thomas's welding and boilermaking skills earn him a place in a skilled workers' team. Every morning, he leaves the confines of the prison with his three workmates. Accompanied by warders, he and his team will be taken all over the extensive prison property, which includes vegetable gardens and an abattoir.

Every so often, as now, Chris pauses and looks intently at me. 'Are you okay? Do you want me to stop?'

The truth – and maybe this is reflected on my face, hence Chris's concern – is that the increasing intimacy I am gaining with Thomas's inner life intensifies my feeling of dread – but not for a second does it make me want to stop.

I shake my head: 'I'm fine. Please go on.'

He nods. 'So, as soon as you leave the confines of the prison, you have so many opportunities. You mingle with the staff. You can charm them by being diligent and smart in your work. And in that position, the staff becomes vulnerable. So for the gang, that becomes an asset. His workmates are also 28s so they work in cahoots, which makes them stronger.'

One of them will have a senior role: either an inspector or a captain. They will worm themselves into that role because it will give them the power to play with the warders' heads. They can get a lot of information about what happens in the lives of the staff and what happens in the outside world because the staff have access to news media. They even befriend the greater Correctional Services community, like their children, because many staff members and their families live on the premises. Walking to and from work, you know, you encounter people.

'Boundaries between prisoners and warders become blurred. They get used to each other, even become friends. The prisoner becomes someone the warder feels he can confide in, vent his anger and frustration to. They become people, rather than just offenders.

'The offender then exploits that, often to the detriment of the staff. They witness their highs and lows and they prey on them, using that knowledge. The workplace becomes a drop-off place. Drugs and cellphones are hidden there. They can make phone calls there.'

The murder itself, as well as Thomas's experience in the *pellepos*, also count in his favour. 'Remember, he already knows The Firm – so that becomes a card to play. And his association with the biggest gang, the 28s, is a feather in his cap. And he has a very good support structure: he gets lots of visits. So he can use that for both his own benefit and for that of the gang.

'At a certain point of his imprisonment, The Firm will contact him and they will reassure him that they will look after him. This relationship is mutually beneficial. You have handed your life over to the 28s and The Firm.

'The Firm will say, Up till now, you did not say you were there in the interests of The Firm; we acknowledge that you kept what little you know under wraps. You may not be aware of it, they will say, but you are under surveillance.'

As I drive home, it is this last sentence that stays with me. So, for Thomas, the stakes of this meeting with me are high. If he gives me the information I seek and this leaks out, the consequences for him could be dire. Do I want a man's life in my hands?

The following afternoon, Chris calls. We have a date for the meeting. Two weeks' time.

17

Preparation

Alan has an important meeting on the date Chris has arranged but he says he will cancel it. I am relieved. I'm not sure I could cope without him at my side.

I play him the recording of my last meeting with Chris so that he has some idea of what to expect. When it comes to the part where Cecil Thomas reveals his role in the gangs as a *wyfie*, Alan exclaims, 'God, it's amazing how frank he is. His position is so humiliating. My instinct would have been to keep quiet about it.'

He listens to the whole recording and then asks to read the court record.

I set about preparing myself. A friend suggests I speak to Sandy Hoffman, a psychologist who has worked with prisoners in Pollsmoor for several years.

I google her and discover that she was driven by a similar tragedy: her brother was murdered, and his killer was never found. Sandy's way of coming to terms with this was to attain a PhD in psychology and then get a job as a psychologist at Pollsmoor, working with convicted murderers, in an attempt to understand what might drive someone to commit such an act. Her attitude is the same as mine: if you bury it, it will eat away at you. Better to confront it and try to understand.

Like me, she comes from a big family, the impact of the murder reverberating through all of them.

I lay before Sandy, one sunny morning at her home in Lakeside, my deep apprehension about the meeting. A tall woman with cropped silver hair and strong, shapely arms emerging from a sleeveless top, she sits me down in an armchair with a cup of strong coffee while I pour out my story. When I begin weeping – which, embarrassingly, is all I seem to be doing these days – she slides a box of tissues onto the arm of my chair.

'What you are doing is very brave,' she says, 'and you deserve credit for it. Carry the confidence of that.'

As to the meeting, her advice is practical: 'Try to see him on his own without warders or spiritual advisers because he will play to them. Try to be alone with him. He must be experiencing enormous darkness and enormous shame – and shame can turn to rage. Authenticity is very important. Look him straight in the eye. Acknowledge him. But don't hope for anything from him. It will make you appear weak and give him power over you. Don't give nice. Don't show fear – fear is like blood to a shark. Be firm; be real. 'Talk about emotions.

Tell him how his actions hurt you, hurt your family.'

Like Chris Malgas, her experience at Pollsmoor is that prisoners want respect and acknowledgement. 'To get his trust, you need to listen to him. Acknowledge him and his rights. Give him a very clear and explicit choice: you can choose to live with your actions, or you can come clean. Whether you wielded the knife or not, you were there. I don't know what part you played but you were witness to a part of my father's life that I need to know about. I'm not interested in guilt or innocence. I want to know what happened.'

I leave her house clutching *Disrespected*, a book she wrote about her 11-year therapeutic relationship with a prisoner called Eddie. I read it that night – it's a fascinating account of her painstaking attempts to help a man deeply damaged by a childhood spent in foster care and orphanages, neglected and horribly abused.

I think, Cecil Thomas might have been beaten by his father, but his life was luxurious compared to Eddie's.

My next meeting is with Irvin Kinnes, whom I have consulted on and off over the past few months. He grew up on the Cape Flats and has a visceral understanding of the gang ecosystem. He has drawn on that to become one of the Cape's most respected intellectuals and policy experts on street and prison gangs. It was Irvin who sent me to Chris Malgas, without whom the meeting with Thomas may never have happened.

Part of the reason I want to see Irvin now is that I know that I will get emotional support as well as practical advice. He is a warm, empathetic man who listens as intently as he talks. We meet in a coffee shop over the road from Parliament, where he now works as an adviser on security issues. It's a serene place, with paintings by local artists on the high white walls and classical music tinkling in the background.

He tells me that I should be very careful about what I reveal. Thomas will have had to get permission from senior members of the 28s to talk to me.

'In prison, they learn how to play people, how to manipulate. Don't give him any information aside from that you are the daughter of his victim. Keep the focus on your father. Don't show fear. Don't blink. Don't move around. Be tough. Be firm.

'Tell yourself you are looking for a story. Be a journalist with him. Say, I'm the daughter of the man you murdered. Why did you do it? That's all I want to know. Remember that you are confronting him. He is not confronting you. Face him down.'

As we part, he says gently, 'Remember, it is just an hour of your life.'

My last meeting is with Liza Grobler. I feel very grateful to Liza. She has been a constant and generous ally. I know that she has worked hard behind the scenes to help get this meeting for me, pushing through the torpor and politics of the prison's bureaucracy.

This time we meet in a coffee shop, in a mall on the other side of the highway from Goodwood Prison. If I could attach a smell to my quest, it would be the warm,

Preparation

acrid smell of coffee. The table where Liza and I sit down, for what will be the final pre-meeting briefing, backs on to shelves packed with bags of coffee from all over the world. From the counter behind us comes the roar and hiss of the coffee machine, churning out cappuccinos, Americanos, lattes.

Liza has been in regular contact with Chris. To the information he provides about Thomas, she adds her own deep understanding of the context.

'You will need to read the situation,' she says. 'It will be very fluid. Be assertive. Don't give him any rope. If he sticks with his story, say, I don't believe you. He has probably done a lot of violent things that he got away with. Don't let him off the hook. Confront him. Be assertive and then compassionate.

'Get him to talk about himself. Point out that he had opportunity. Press his buttons – his vulnerable points, like his mother and his status. Why did he enter through the silver line? They become victims immediately. They are not highly regarded. They are not brave. They are powerless and treated like shit. He is a sex slave and a maid, assigned to some older guy. And use the leverage of parole.

'Ask him why the murder was so violent. Was he stabbing his own father? Say, How did you feel when you were finished?'

He is a typical case of having been beaten bad, she says. He is staying stuck in the narrative because he is ashamed. He disassociates from the act.

Lying in bed with Alan that night, I say, 'The problem with this victim–offender dialogue paradigm is that it pigeonholes me as a victim. Being a victim intimates passivity, a lack of agency, someone to whom things are done. "Victim–offender" means you are locked into a relationship with the person who has harmed you. I need another word.'

'Wounded,' he says. 'You are not a victim. You are wounded.'

I'm delighted with this – wounded is what I am! It implies transience, fluidity. Wounds can be healed. I can heal myself.

18

Voorberg

The evening before I am due to meet Cecil Thomas, my chief concern is what to wear. I want to appear businesslike, but not too formal – as if I have made an effort. Mostly, though, what I want is to show as little flesh as possible. It helps that it is winter, so I am able to wear long pants and a long-sleeved shirt buttoned up to the neck.

That night I barely sleep, going over and over in my mind the advice I have received, trying to work out how I can use it in a way that feels comfortable for me. But the whole situation is so far beyond anything I have experienced or expected to experience that the image that stays with me as I finally drift into sleep is that of a rabbit caught in the headlights, frantically darting this way and that, unable to escape the vehicle of doom bearing down on me.

At 5.30 a.m, when I wake Alan, it is still dark. And cold. I put on the clothes I have laid out the night before and, over them, a jacket that covers my hips and thighs. My hair I tie back into a tight ponytail.

We pick Chris up outside the Cullinan Hotel on the Foreshore, where his son has dropped him off, and head down the N1. I get into the back and Chris takes the passenger seat beside Alan, who is driving. Traffic is light until we approach the turnoff to Gouda, where they are resurfacing the road and a stop-and-go halts our lane of traffic for an achingly slow 10 minutes.

I think back to my first trip to Voorberg three months earlier, that naïve, hopeful first stop on this fraught journey. When I had simply made an appointment with the governor and asked him to set up a meeting with Cecil Thomas. The traffic was a lot heavier then.

I mention this and, like Patricia, Chris once more expresses his astonishment that I went in there alone, with no preparation and no backup. The gangs would have known all about my visit, he says. They would have asked the warders who you were and what you were doing there. Voorberg is run by the gangs.

Was this, I wonder with hindsight, why my direct approach didn't work?

Chris changes gear into facilitator-speak: 'How did you feel afterwards? Give me a colour!' Pink, I reply. Like a new dawn. I had felt so hopeful, then after Pastor Zimri's warm welcome and his promise to set the meeting in motion. A false dawn, as it turned out.

He asks how I am feeling now and I say my biggest fear is that I will start to cry, which would be humiliating and I would feel I had lost face and therefore any control over what transpired between us.

Chris tries to reassure me: 'It's a strength to show emotion. He mustn't change you. Don't let him take away what you are,' he urges. 'Who you are.'

He also says I must not show fear, which, frankly, will be equally hard.

I need to feel safe, he says. I must be confident that he will keep me safe.

As with my first visit, we are much too early for our appointment so we drive past the gates of Voorberg and on to Porterville. In the same smoky, hungover pub we order breakfast. Chris and Alan eat heartily, hungry after our early start. I push away my plate of eggs and toast, too wound up to eat. The coffee, hot and strong, provides a welcome jolt.

Shortly before 9 a.m., we retrace our steps and drive through the Voorberg gates. Chris guides us through the entry protocols, greeting warders left and right, easing our way in. They don't even search us. I could have smuggled anything in. I regret for a moment having followed instructions not to bring my iPhone, the mode of recording I am most comfortable with. Instead, I have an old recorder.

In the small reception office, Chris introduces us to the warder on duty, explaining sotto voce that this warder has been relegated to reception because he was stabbed by a prisoner a couple of weeks ago and is still too traumatised to work inside the prison.

The man himself says nothing, just silently turns his face to reveal the wound on the left side. It is a vividly red, swollen ridge a couple of centimetres long, horribly close to his eye.

We follow Chris out of the reception area and wait for someone to collect us. Chris's mind is still on the wounded man. 'It was so sudden. He was speaking to an offender and another one came up behind him and the warder was only alerted to this when the offender he was talking to raised his eyes. The warder lifted his left arm but he was too late. The guy slashed the side of his face. There had been three guys behind him but when he looked around again, they were all gone. He was in shock. Because it happens like a machine.

'In prison, they always stab your face because every time you look in the mirror you will see the scar and that is a psychological triumph. Long after, you still see the mark.'

He shakes his head and tells me again, 'Voorberg is one of the most dangerous prisons in the Cape because it is run by the gangs on the mythology of Po Mabaso.'

Our escort arrives, introducing himself as a pastor and 'moral and spiritual adviser', and explaining that he will facilitate the meeting in the absence of Zimri who is (surprise, surprise!) not available. We follow him down a long corridor into a large, open-plan space with a series of smaller rooms down one side. On the opposite side, a few prisoners are ironing clothes. The first couple of rooms appear to be classrooms, with men in orange overalls sitting at desks facing a teacher who is writing on a blackboard.

The pastor informs us that he is taking us to meet the social worker who will also be present at the meeting. Her office is just beyond the classrooms, but when we get there it is empty and the pastor goes off to find her. While we wait, we are approached by a young man with long black dreadlocks. He is slim and fragile-looking but bright as a peacock with blue eyeshadow fringed by a thick line of kohl, his cheeks and lips a rosy pink. Chris introduces himself and us and asks what he is in for. Six years, for house-breaking, he reveals.

I mutter to Chris: surely such a man is very vulnerable here?

He will be the wife of a powerful gang member who will protect him, replies Chris. He will be okay.

The pastor returns with the social worker, a sleekly groomed young woman. She first takes us into her office and then, between them, they decide it is not an appropriate venue for the meeting as 'offenders walk in and out'. It all feels slightly chaotic, as if our visit was neither prepared for nor wanted.

This dithering amplifies a sense of not being contained, not being safe, but I feel fatalistic about it. At least we are here, at least it is finally happening. That is all that matters now.

The pastor leads us down further long corridors,

through gates that have to be unlocked and then locked again behind us, until we reach what appears to be a small boardroom. It is windowless and empty aside from four small tables pushed together, and a few chairs on either side.

The pastor and the social worker leave to fetch Thomas.

Chris snaps into action, choreographing the setting in which the confrontation will take place. He asks Alan to help him and, together, they pull apart the four small tables and push two together. These will form the barrier between the two parties. On the one side, facing the door, he arranges three chairs: I must occupy the one in the centre, he says, with Alan on my left and Chris himself on my right, closest to the door.

On the table I set out my recorder. Alan places the printout of the court record in front of him.

We have already decided which roles each of us will play. Alan, the academic, will be the forensic analyst; Chris, former warder and gang expert, will be the director and hard man. I, the 'victim', will be the voice of suffering, of reproach and potential redemption.

Our strategy is that I will focus on my central quest: what happened in that house that night? How and why did my father die? Chris will circle his vulnerable areas – his mother and his position of humiliation as *wyfie* within the gang – in an attempt to break down his defences. Alan, who has studied the court record, will add the forensic evidence, intervening wherever he sees fit.

We expect the meeting to be fluid and dynamic. We will need to be agile and alert, adapting as we go to whatever comes our way. We know that Thomas is still maintaining his innocence. But we are hoping that, at this meeting, we will force a breakthrough and finally get to the truth.

At 10.20 a.m., Thomas is brought in.

19

The meeting

Chris directs Thomas to the chair opposite me. The pastor sits down on his right, the social worker on his left.

It is a shock to see him but I force myself to look. He looks much better than he had at the trial, eight years before. He has lost that hunched, harried look. He appears bigger, stronger, clear-complexioned, with short, pale-brown hair. Alan says afterwards that he reminded him of Kevin Spacey.

Chris introduces me and Alan. We greet him and I thank him for agreeing to meet with us. I ask his permission to record the meeting. He nods. Yes, it's fine.

'You look well!' remarks Chris in Afrikaans.

Thomas smiles nervously, stammers: 'I exercise a lot. I play rugby.' Then, as if apologising: 'It's a privilege to play rugby. I know it's a privilege.'

Niceties over, I draw a deep breath and begin with my prepared statement: 'I'm here to get the truth of my father's murder. I want to make it clear that if I get the truth today about what happened in his house that night, I will ask my family to support your attempts at parole when you become eligible in five years' time. If I don't get the truth, my family will not support parole.'

I have rehearsed this moment and I know that, for maximum impact, I have to look directly at him as I say this. I can't falter or drop my eyes. I can't show fear. But the sight of him, just a couple of metres away, looking straight at me, takes me back to the horror of the courtroom and I feel myself struggling to breathe. The room, windowless and airless, feels as if it is closing in on me. Under cover of the table, Alan takes my hand and squeezes it. I concentrate on the warmth and strength of his grip and start to breathe again.

According to his niece, Thomas misses his children and desperately wants to be close to them, especially as they enter their teens. The victim's family's opinion weighs heavily in parole hearings. He must know this. I am offering him the possibility of a life again, where he can be a free man, watching his children grow up.

Thomas nods. Yes, he says, I will tell the truth.

Stammering badly, he says in Afrikaans, 'I will start at the beginning. On 9 August, I went to Bellville to do some shopping. I bumped into Llewellyn Tobias and I told him I was now living in Saron. He asked if I would like to go with him to Worcester on Monday …'

I feel despair welling up, mixed with rage. What is the bloody point of all this if we just get these lies all over again?

Alan interrupts him: 'We want to hear what happened that night, not this story again.' He points at the court record lying open in front of him, pretends to read. 'Here it says, the judge did not believe that story. We do not believe that story!'

Silence. Chris fills it, saying gently, 'Tell us about your relationship with your mother. Was it good?' It takes me a moment to realise that this intervention is strategic.

Thomas nods. 'It was very good. She always supported me. We lived with my grandmother and my mother worked full-time in the canning factory. My grandmother was also good to me. And my sisters.'

Chris goes in harder now, touching on a more painful subject: 'And your father?'

A different expression crosses Thomas's face, a darker one. When he begins speaking again, the stammer is more pronounced. The halting, painful delivery contrasts strongly with the physical strength he emanates.

'My father was a carpenter. He made furniture and he worked all over the place. The last few years he worked in Worcester. He wasn't home a lot.'

Chris: 'How was your relationship with him?'

Thomas: 'He drank wine but he wasn't difficult in the house. He didn't hit my mother but he was very hard on me. My job was to look after the chickens and clean out

The meeting

the chicken *hok*. That was my peaceful place. When I forgot to clean it, he used to hit me. That is where I went to cry when my father hit me. When I stammered, he would hit me on the head. I always stammered!

'I felt I could not satisfy my father. Only if I didn't stammer, didn't make mistakes, was I good enough. Sometimes I hated my father. My father picked on me. I felt like I was the black sheep.'

Chris takes the court record from Alan and makes a show of opening it up, looking for a certain page. Thomas watches him, apprehensive.

Looking up, Chris reads from the judgment: 'The judge says you were inside the murder house when you made phone calls from Mr McGregor's phone to your friend, Neil Prins. You then took the goods to Saron and you tried to sell the camera and the car.'

Thomas is vigorously shaking his head. The phone was brought to him when he was sitting outside in the car, he insists. He was told to call Neil Prins in Saron and tell him that he must come and fetch 'the goods' at the petrol station in Tulbagh.

Chris: 'Where were you when Mr McGregor was stabbed?'

Thomas: 'I was outside in the car.'

Alan cuts in with a reference to my father's neighbour. 'Let's go back. Nelia said you were wearing gloves when you came to ask her where the house was – it wasn't cold. Why were you wearing gloves if not because you didn't want to leave fingerprints?'

Thomas: 'I wasn't wearing gloves.'

This is getting nowhere.

Alan: 'How did you feel with the gangsters in the car? Why did you get into the car when you saw the gangsters had a gun?'

Thomas: 'I only saw the gun when we were in the car outside the house. I was afraid that they would shoot me.'

Chris: 'How do you explain the fact that Mr McGregor's blood and your blood were found on your sock?'

Thomas responds with the same ridiculous answer he gave in court. The unnamed gangsters who committed the murder swapped clothes with him. That was how my father's blood had seeped into his sock. After he was arrested, the police took all his clothes except for his socks. These were only taken a few days later, after the police had beaten him up. This story had been demolished in court.

The small, airless room is tight with tension. On our side of the table, a growing frustration and despair. From Thomas, obduracy, and the undertones of a whining self-pity beginning to emerge under the crossfire of questions. The complications of communication: Chris speaks Afrikaans; Alan and I speak mostly English, but also some Afrikaans; the pastor, who speaks no Afrikaans, is straining to follow. Thomas speaks in a painfully slow, stuttering Afrikaans, frequently so quietly I can barely hear him.

The meeting

I want to ask for a glass of water but I'm afraid of breaking the momentum.

I take a deep breath: time for a low blow. 'This is a difficult question,' I say, looking steadily at him. 'But I need to ask it. When you were stabbing my father, was it really your own father you were stabbing?'

He begins weeping and says in English, looking directly back at me, 'I did not stab your father. Honestly, I did not stab your father. Why must I lie to you? After 10 years? There were hard times. Why must I still lie to you?'

Alan reminds him that he said that if he told the truth, The Firm had threatened to harm his mother. This would be a reason not to tell the truth.

Thomas insists he is now telling the truth. 'When I got to the court, my family was all there. This is why I sometimes got confused and told lies.'

The pastor turns to him and says gently, 'You have nothing to lose now. The truth will set you free. Maybe you have also told your mother and your brother and sisters that you didn't do this thing and now you say you did it?'

'I didn't do it.'

Chris explodes: 'Cecil, it is now 11.20. At 10.20 you said you would be very truthful with us!'

There is a brief silence. Then Chris starts up again, this time on his gang connections.

Chris: 'Do you belong to a gang?'

Thomas: 'At school, I belonged to the Vatos Locos.

When I was 14 or 15, we watched a movie about Vatos Locos. *Blood In Blood Out.* We were a group of friends who went around together. At that age, we liked girls; we liked nice clothes to attract the girls. Also, there was another gang called the Bad Boys.'

I interject: 'Was there an initiation?'

Thomas: 'A tattoo – VL – on my upper left arm. My mother saw the tattoo and she didn't like it because she didn't want me to belong to a gang. I said we weren't a gang. The Bad Boys carried knives but we didn't.'

Chris reminds him that he had a conviction at the time for possession of a dangerous weapon.

Thomas answers, 'He attacked my friend first. I chased him with a panga. I saw my friend lying with a knife sticking out of his head. I chased him a panga I found on the road. He is my friend. I must help him! Then my mother sent me to live with my aunt and niece in Kraaifontein because I was involved in drinking and involved in violence.'

Abruptly, Chris changes direction.

'What does "*Hosh my bru*" mean to you?' He is referring to the greeting that Thomas claimed the two gangsters used when he first met them – the two men he refuses to name..

'It is a 26 prison gang greeting.'

Chris: 'What does the word "*gazielam*" mean to you?'

Thomas: 'We are blood brothers.'

Alan: 'You said in the trial that you started using tik

in 2006. Was your need to get tik a factor?'

No response.

Chris: 'Llewellyn Tobias took you to the *pellepos* where they gave you a safe haven to smoke?'

Thomas: 'Yes. Llewellyn is a gangster. He was from The Firm. The Firm belongs to Langkop. The Firm is not only 26, it is also 27. I heard in the court that Llewellyn Tobias was a 28.'

Chris: 'And now?'

Thomas: 'I am a 28. I am a private. My work is to *sabela*.'

Chris: 'You are a *wyfie*.'

Thomas looks down, clearly upset, stammering so badly he can hardly get it out. 'Yes, I am a *wyfie*.' He does not want to go there. His sense of shame is palpable.

The social worker pats his shoulder and says in a motherly tone, 'Cecil, *ons is nie jou vyand nie*' ('we are not your enemy').

Chris: 'Are you British? What is your uniform?'

Thomas hesitates and then starts slowly, gazing past us, as if somewhere else. A kind of peace infuses him as if, trance-like, he's going inside himself and it's a place that centres him and restores him to who he is. The stammer almost disappears. It's a remarkable transformation from the harried, distressed man of a few seconds earlier.

'My shoes are white takkies. I wear white socks and shoes and shorts and a belt with a silver buckle decorated with a flower to show everything you do is beautiful.

Top two buttons. First is closed to show discipline and respect. Second is open to show I am always available. I have a white beret, also with a flower on it.'

Chris presses him: 'The one button is undone because it means you must be ready 24/7 for your husband to have sex with you? And the flower means you are beautiful?'

He nods.

Chris: 'What drugs can you get in prison?'

'Tik, dagga. And pills.'

'Heroin?'

'I haven't seen heroin.'

Me: 'Tell us about your work. Are you paid?'

'I began on R48 a month. Now I am paid R96 a month. There are four of us in the work team. All of us are 28s. The supervisor is called Mr Zola.'

Chris: 'Where is your father now?'

'My father died when I was 14. On his deathbed, for the first time, I told him I loved him. And he told me he loved me.'

I burst out: 'Why did you have to kill my father? He was naked, old, defenceless. Why couldn't you just take his things and leave him alone? Where does the violence come from? You have a loving family. You had opportunities they didn't have. Where does this violence come from? You stabbed him 25 times.'

He just looks at me: 'I didn't kill him.'

And then he says something strange. Almost as if correcting me, he says, 'He was stabbed 24 times. In

The meeting

court they said it was one person who did the murder. The advocate said there were stab wounds on the torso. How can one person logically do that? There must have been a second person to hold him back. Otherwise, you would have had to cuff him or hold his hands behind his back.' He clenches his right fist, as if he is holding something, and then makes quick, vicious downward jabs. I find it chilling. It looks so automatic, so practised.

Alan is looking at the post-mortem record. 'Yes, there is a bruise on his left wrist. It could be from someone holding him.'

The pastor interrupts and, addressing Chris, says, 'Can we talk in the corridor?'

When they come back in, Chris says it is after 1 p.m. and the prison is being locked up for the day. The pastor is afraid we will be locked in too if we don't leave now. Later Chris tells us that the prisoners are given both lunch and supper at 1 p.m. and are then locked into their cells until 7 a.m.

I feel the energy seeping out of me. It has been an intense, exhausting three hours in this comfortless cell of a room. This moment feels like defeat. We have got nowhere.

But it is important to observe the courtesies.

I look at Thomas and say, dully, 'Thank you for agreeing to see me.'

He looks directly at me and says in English, 'I am very sorry for your pain but I did not murder your father. Even if I have to sit here for the full 30 years, I will, because I can't confess to a crime I did not commit.'

It feels as rehearsed as my opening statement to him.

The pastor leads us out back through the maze of corridors, silent and empty now that the prisoners have been locked into their cells. At the exit, we say goodbye to the wounded warder. He nods, his face averted so that his scarred side is in shadow.

20

What I've learnt

The morning after the meeting, I wake early from a deep, exhausted sleep with questions pulsing through my brain. Loose ends are dangling everywhere and they must be tied off. I say to Alan, dozing beside me, 'I'm going to ask Chris to arrange another meeting.'

He opens his eyes, alert now. 'Yes. You must!' The previous evening, he was dissecting Cecil Thomas's answers, comparing them to the court record, analysing the gaps and inconsistencies. He too has a list.

I call Chris and arrange to meet.

At 10.00 a.m. the next day, we are ensconced at our usual table, near the passage leading to the toilets at Martins. I blurt out my request: 'We need to see Cecil Thomas again. There are still so many things we need to ask him.'

Chris doesn't answer for a moment. Then he says,

slowly, that he will try to arrange a meeting if I want it, but that I need to think hard about whether it would be worth it.

'You must assume you will never get the truth,' he says gently. 'He won't reveal it because he has sold himself to the gang. Blood in, blood out. He entered through blood and it is his blood that will be shed if he tries to leave.

'He is still embedded in his own suffering, in his drug abuse and his allegiance to the gang. They would not take it well if he told you what really happened. He did reveal the operational head of the mission – Llewellyn Tobias – but because of Tobias's gang seniority and possibly because of his connections with the police, it was Thomas who took the fall.'

Chris has touched on something that has always puzzled me. Chris Langkop and Ernest Arendse's drug-dealing operation was well known to one of the country's major crime-fighting operations stationed just a few kilometres away. How could this possibly happen? Why hadn't it been shut down?

Chris shrugs. This is dangerous territory. He points to the recent arrest of senior policemen for collusion with gang leaders. 'Who do you trust?'

He doesn't need to spell it out. I know how widespread police corruption is; how savvy gangsters play smoke and mirrors with senior cops, until it is hard to tell one side from the other.

As we part, possibly for the last time, I say, 'Chris, can I hug you?'

He stands there, stiff as a soldier, as I clasp my arms around him. Proper to the end, he gives an embarrassed little laugh and says, 'Send my regards to Alan!'

I walk along the sea's edge, feeling the adrenaline that has driven me for so long begin to ebb. I realise that the bottom line is that I can't face another meeting with Thomas. It was just too frustrating, too stressful. And pointless, in that I failed to get the answers I sought.

I tell Alan what Chris said: that the gang had instructed Cecil Thomas what to say and that if he diverged from it, he would be punished, possibly killed. Alan agrees that we should drop it. Neither of us wants a man's death on our conscience. And who knows what danger it would open us to.

I question myself: Why was my father's murder so devastating? It's not as if, like my friend, I've lost a child. My father was 79. Even the youngest of us, his children, were approaching middle age. This could hardly equate to the irrecoverable loss of someone still umbilically attached.

I think it was primarily the shock of it. My father had a talent for reinvention. He would go through periods of deep despondency and then emerge, full of vigour, bursting with ideas for some great new venture. He always said that he never planned, financially or otherwise, more than six months ahead.

At 79, he still had a good decade left in him. He was emerging from the sadness of my mother's illness and death and envisioning a new, different life. This was not some sad, sick old man. He was still vigorous, still up for adventure.

I think, now, that my quest was naïve. Despite all the warnings, I held on to the hope that all would be okay in the end. That I would be able to express eloquently how important it was to me to know what happened to my father in his last hours and that, in the face of this, Thomas would undergo a Damascene conversion and confess all. We might weep together. It would be a profound, dramatic purging for both of us – my anger, my grief; his guilt and shame – and, both of us, freed of this awful load, would be able to walk, calmer and lighter, into a newly imagined future.

But, in my blind rush to confront, I had ignored reality. On a purely practical level, what was in it for Cecil Thomas? It's been abundantly clear that there will be no support for him to follow a different path. That this was a tick-box exercise for the prison to get a tiresome woman off its back.

There'd be nothing waiting to embrace a repentant sinner. He would be taken straight back to his communal cell, in which he'd be locked until breakfast the next morning – for what, 17 hours? His only debriefing would be from gang leaders. To survive, the only story he could have told was the one that had, in fact, transpired – he had stuck, against all odds, to the tired, implausible story he had told in court.

In the months that follow, as I ponder the visit, it strikes me that the whole thing has been something of a farce. Despite all the grand words in the Constitution and in the legislation. The lofty ideals, expressed with such agility, of the principle of restorative justice that theoretically underpins our system are just that – ideals.

If my encounter with Cecil Thomas were to have any chance of success, a system would have to be in place. Efficient, ethical governance would have been required. He would have to be offered a credible alternative life, away from the gang, and treatment for his drug addiction.

And when he leaves prison, what will be waiting for a convicted murderer, even a repentant one? If he comes clean and my family supports parole and he is released in 2023, he will only be in his forties. But with his tattoos and his prison record, who will give him a job? Especially in a country where one in three adults is jobless. How will he find his way into an honest, respectable life?

The court case, with my father's murderer convicted and sent to prison for the foreseeable future, should have been a catharsis of sorts for us, a conclusion to a ghastly chapter. Instead, it was just a beginning. Thomas was dispatched to an institution where his criminal career would be developed and honed. When he is finally freed, it is likely he will be a greater threat to society than he was when he was imprisoned.

I think, now, that possibly my father was right in

his conviction about looming retribution. Although he would have had no inkling of where it would have come from: that his nemesis would take this stealthy, subterranean form, and not the bloody, chaotic riots of his imagination, fuelled by his experiences at Glendale.

A guerrilla war had claimed his life and it had been a long time coming.

The Number gangs seem to me to be the distillation of the dehumanisation cemented into the foundations of modern South Africa. They are immune to the Mandela miracle, far too dark and deep to be touched by his sweeping light.

Today's prison cells, fetid, crowded, conspiratorial, have become the caves from which Po Mabaso and Nongoloza plotted and organised their gangs of bandits to go out and plunder and steal, in return for which they'd find everything they needed: food, guns, drugs and, above all else, a powerful mythology to give their lives meaning.

They spill out of the prisons, exploiting the space opened up in this gentler, more humane era. Whereas before Nongoloza's children stole the hard-won wages of migrant mineworkers, today they enslave the poor and vulnerable by getting them hooked on drugs. They have merged with the ever-growing criminal underworld. They poison the democratic order by corrupting policemen and warders and politicians. They turn townships into war zones and don't care about the innocents killed in the crossfire. They organise hits on unsuspecting civilians to steal their silver and gold.

After the murder and the trial, I saw hooded assassins around every corner. Now, it is not personal. I have become increasingly aware of the shadow world that underlies our seemingly neat and ordered one. When I eat out at a restaurant, with the sun on my back, the delicious locally grown food and the intoxicating local wines, I think about the gangs blackmailing the owner for protection money. When I read about yet another murder, I think of the family left behind, shocked, bewildered, grief-stricken, like us. And left largely to their own devices, to deal with their trauma on their own.

In the years during which I laboured over this book, frequently having to take a break because the immersion in these painful events was just too much, I was often asked whether it was worth it. My answer is unequivocally yes. It meant shining a light into a dark corner where monsters lurked and finding a damaged, frightened man. More than that, tracing his trajectory gave me an insight into the underground forces that fracture and warp our country.

But it also frightened me. Because now I see how the violence upon which this country was founded still permeates and defines it. It was only in London, where we were spending a few months, that I found the distance and courage to finish this manuscript at last.

It's a difficult thing, this. I feel totally bound up with my country. It's what made me. Its pain and its anger and its yearnings are mine too. When I've spent time in the UK, I begin to long anew for South Africa's intensity – the ferocity of the sun, the ferocity of its passions. I also feel some responsibility to help make things right.

The weight of race hasn't changed that much – the colour of one's skin is still a major signifier of historical privilege, with all the resentment it attracts and the guilt that comes with it. Racist white people assume I'm one of them before I've even opened my mouth. It's a prickly badge to wear.

It comes to me that what I really wanted from this quest was to hear my father's voice one more time. Many, many times, I have tried to imagine him describing the events leading to his death. He always used to construct little stories out of things that happened to him: light, amusing, with a side of self-deprecation. But in this, what would have been his final instalment, all I can really grasp is his opening sentence: 'When I saw those buggers, I …' I imagine that, for as long as he was able, he would have kept up an internal monologue, fashioning a story out of it to tell us afterwards.

If Thomas had described the attack truthfully – including how my father responded – I could have filled in my father's voice. I could have heard him one last time. It would have been a kind of goodbye.

This is the final loss. And now I must let go of it.

Epilogue

On 21 March 2020, Alan and I got married. Our initial thoughts were of a registry office wedding, followed by a lunch at a wine farm with 30-odd friends and family.

People, we discovered, love a wedding and, almost without our noticing it, it became a big wedding. By January 2020, it had become a destination wedding, with 100 guests coming from all over South Africa and beyond. We decided to have it in Arniston, in the Fishermen's Union hall, close to the harbour. It is a place with rich cultural and historical associations: a monument to the successful struggle by Arniston's fisher community to resist apartheid-era attempts to force them from their homes on prime beachfront land. It is also testament to their profound bond with the sea which, through bad times and good, has given them a living.

The hall is very pretty but not very large. We hired an adjoining stretch tent with a dance floor, extra chairs and tables and glasses and plates. We ordered dozens of fishcakes from a fisher family and lambs on the spit for the red-meat eaters. We bought gallons of wine and beer and Liza made us a giant fruit cake surrounded by a flotilla of silvery white cupcakes.

Most of our guests decided to make a weekend of it and Arniston's accommodation was rapidly booked up. Andrew was to host a cocktail party in his courtyard the night before and we organised guided walks for those new to Arniston on the Saturday and Sunday mornings.

The cherry on the top was that Michael Weeder, dean of St George's Cathedral, agreed to drive down from Cape Town and marry us in the hall. The fact that we were a non-observant Jew and a lapsed Catholic with no links to Anglicanism didn't faze this generous-spirited man of God.

And then COVID-19 struck and, within days, all our carefully laid plans fell apart.

On 15 March, six days before the wedding, a grave-faced President Cyril Ramaphosa announced on TV that a national state of disaster had been declared.

Travellers from high-risk countries such as the UK and US were banned from entering the country. Domestic travel was strongly discouraged. From 26 March, five days after our wedding was due to be held, the whole country was to go into lockdown, with no one allowed to leave their homes, except to get food or medicine.

Epilogue

We were thrown into a panic. The wedding was still legally permissible, but would it be irresponsible to go ahead? What if, god forbid, it went down in history as a superspreader event? We agonised over it, veering from one position to another.

Meanwhile, the cancellations were coming in thick and fast. Firstly, all our overseas guests – including my brother Simon and his family from the UK, Alan's brother from Australia, and my cousins from the US. Every half hour there was a new SMS, email or WhatsApp from hitherto committed guests regretfully withdrawing.

A couple of friends sternly advised us to cancel. Others urged us to go ahead. We thought of the faithful few who still intended to be there, who had already forked out for travel and accommodation, including my 83-year-old uncle and aunt who had flown in from Monaco a week before the ban.

Above all, we wanted to go ahead. We wanted to be married. Who knows how long this damn thing would last? And when would we get to party again?

The hall was ruled out – it was already clear that the virus spread through the air and a large number of people in a confined space was not a good idea.

As the week progressed, a great, gorgeous silver lining emerged. Nature, it appeared, was on our side. The sun shone. And kept on shining. The wind, usually a pushy, persistent presence, kept its distance. Predictions for the weekend looked better and better. On the

Wednesday, Cathy, staring at the barometer, said, 'We can do it on the beach.'

I phoned Michael Weeder, who had remained supportive throughout despite having to deal with his own impossible dilemmas of how to continue to serve his large flock. He could marry us on the beach, he said, as long as there was some sort of cover over our heads and his.

My brother-in-law dug an ancient canvas canopy out the storeroom and he and my nephews set it up with the help of a couple of makeshift poles, ropes and some large rocks. They entwined white king proteas and ribbon around the ropes and made a makeshift path to an imaginary altar, edged with shells and smooth, white stones.

We were married in the late afternoon under a blue sky with an indigo sea sighing and murmuring behind us. There were about fifty guests in the end, all dressed up in bright summer clothes, clustered around the canopy and perched on the lower reaches of Lovers' Rock, appropriately situated alongside it.

Giddy with delight and relief, afterwards, we drank champagne and ate fish cakes, and then wandered over to the house of a kind friend who had offered to host the dinner and dancing in her capacious back garden.

In the end it was better than anything we had imagined – a joyous, spontaneous, intimate wedding, a memory to sustain us through the long, dark months that were to follow. And no one got sick.

Newlyweds Liz McGregor and Alan Hirsch

—

Looking at the photographs while writing this, I notice one of myself hurling something into the sea and remember what it was: a protea for my parents, now out there, somewhere in the beautiful universe.

Acknowledgements

Jeremy Boraine, Charles Siboto, Jean-Marie Korff and the rest of the team at Jonathan Ball have, as ever, been a joy to work with. Angela Voges edited my manuscript with great sensitivity and intelligence. Thank you.

Early readers Haiyao Zheng, Francis Gerard, Barbara Erasmus and Bridget Pitt provided brilliant suggestions for improvement of the manuscript at critical junctures, as well as much-needed support.

My Scottish cousin, Peter Cairns, was an invaluable source of information about our mutual ancestors, and his wife Lesley fed us spectacular meals.

Criminologist Chris Giffard generously shared his library, his contacts and his knowledge.

I'm also indebted, for various kindnesses, to Jonathan Hyslop, Zelda Holtzman, Keith Breckenridge, Andrew Faull, Elrena van der Spuy, Sarah Nuttall, Bonita

Bennett, Don Pinnock, Madeleine Bunting and Philippa Skowno.

To all the helpful and knowledgeable librarians I have consulted, including Judith Legg at the Aberdeen Central Library, Julia Woolcott at the Barloworld archives, Zofia Solej at the William Cullen Library at the University of the Witwatersrand, Pam Hutchinson at the Chamber of Mines archives, and the team at Special Collections at the University of Cape Town, I am very grateful.

And finally, Alan, my soul mate, who has kept me going through many a crisis of confidence and courage over the past four years – you know what you mean to me.

Glossary

impi: A group of Zulu warriors, usually armed with shields and spears

Karoo: An arid, semi-desert region in the interior of South Africa

leiwater: Afrikaans for 'channelled water', a system of channelling irrigation water via open furrows to farms, smallholdings or gardens from a nearby water source such as a dam or river. It works on a rotation basis, with properties in different areas taking turns to receive the water, hence the alternative name *'waterbeurt'* – a *beurt* is a turn.

lekker: Afrikaans for 'nice', an anglicised term in South Africa

patat: Afrikaans for 'sweet potato'. Robert Shell's wonderful, searing book on slavery in South Africa, *Children of Bondage: A Social History of the Slave*

Society at the Cape of Good Hope, 1652–1838, seems to confirm that 'Patat' was a nickname given to slaves:

> The settlers' facetious spirit found its fullest expression in ridiculous or pejorative nicknames given to slaves, faithfully copied in the transfers. The most common name was Fortune (Fortuijn), presumably an ironical reminder of where household wealth lay. Pickle Herring was the nickname of one slave; Winter Butter was another, a racial joke referring to the slave's pale skin colour. The list is as endless as it is demeaning. Thickleg (Dikbeen), Long-time-coming (Lang onderweg) Watch-out (Pasop), Sweet Potato (Patat), Teawater (Theewater), Blixem (Buckslam – an expletive), Welcome (Wellekom), Sabbath Ape-child (Domingo Aapkind), or simply Ape (Aap), Evil (Slegt), Clever (Slim), and Servidor and Shitato, which require as little translation as they require imagination.
>
> Presumably thigh-slapping humor was explained, or perhaps the joke grew old, but the names stuck. When the slave was sold again the name reappeared in the records.

takkies: South African term for sneakers or sports shoes
wors: Afrikaans for 'sausage', an anglicised term in South Africa

References

THE TRIAL

Dolley, Caryn. (2019). *The Enforcers: Inside Cape Town's Deadly Nightclub Battles*. Cape Town: Jonathan Ball Publishers.

Faull, Andrew. (2009). Recruitment, Integrity and Allegations of Torture Against the Hawks. Polity, 14 October 2009. Available at https://www.polity.org.za/article/recruitment-integrity-and-allegations-of-torture-against-the-hawks-2009-10-14 (accessed 13 December 2021).

Faull, Andrew. (2018). *Police Work and Identity: A South African Ethnography*. Abingdon: Routledge.

Kinnes, Irvin. (2000). Monograph No 48: From urban street gangs to criminal empires – The changing face of gangs in the Western Cape. Available at https://media.africaportal.org/documents/Mono48.pdf (accessed

13 December 2021).

Kinnes, Irvin. (2017). *Contested Governance: Police and Gang Interactions*. PhD thesis, University of Cape Town.

Nombembe, Philani. (2019). Cape Flats 'reign of terror' culminates in trial for the Terrible Josters. *TimesLIVE*, 6 May 2019. Available at https://www.timeslive.co.za/news/south-africa/2019-05-06-cape-flats-reign-of-terror-culminates-in-trial-for-the-terrible-josters/ (accessed 13 December 2021).

Pinnock, Don. (2016). *Gang Town*. Cape Town: Tafelberg.

Shell, Robert Carl-Heinz. (1994). *Children of Bondage: A Social History of the Slave Society at the Cape of Good Hope 1652–1838*. Middletown, CT: Wesleyan University Press.

WEAVING IT ALL TOGETHER

Ascherson, Neal. (2002). *Stone Voices: The Search for Scotland*. London: Granta Books.

Bunting, Madeleine. (2017). *Love of Country: A Hebridean Journey*. London: Granta Books.

Devine, Tom. (2011). *To the Ends of the Earth: Scotland's Global Diaspora 1750–2010*. Washington, D.C.: Smithsonian Books.

Hyslop, Jonathan. (2005). *The Notorious Syndicalist: J.T. Bain – A Scottish Rebel in Colonial South Africa*. Johannesburg: Jacana.

Hyslop, Jonathan. (2006). Making Scotland in South

Africa: Charles Murray, the Transvaal's Aberdeenshire Poet. In David Lambert and Alan Lester (eds). *Colonial Lives Across the British Empire: Imperial Careering in the Long Nineteenth Century*. Cambridge: Cambridge University Press, pp. 309–334.

Lockhart, Douglas. (2001). Lotted lands and planned villages in north-east Scotland. *Agricultural History Review* 49(1): 17–40.

Mackenzie, John M and Dalziel, Nigel. (2012). *The Scots in South Africa: Ethnicity, Identity, Gender and Race, 1772–1914*. Manchester: Manchester University Press.

Penny, Cecilia. (2000). *Stuartfield Our Place*. Stuartfield: Stuartfield Millennium Group.

The Press and Journal. (1974). Stuartfield: Beauty of a Buchan village. *The Press and Journal*, 30 November 1974.

ALEXANDER AND NONGOLOZA

Department of Justice. (1912). Nongoloza's testimony. *Department of Justice Annual Report for the Year 1912*, pp. 237–240.

Guy, Jeff. (1994). *The Destruction of the Zulu Kingdom: The Civil War in Zululand, 1879–1884*. Durban: University of Natal Press.

Katz, Elaine. (1978). Silicosis on Witwatersrand Gold Mines with Particular Reference to the Miners' Phthisis Commission of 1902 to 1903 (Paper 2). Johannesburg: University of the Witwatersrand.

Mostert, Noel. (1992). *Frontiers: The Epic of South*

Africa's Creation and the Tragedy of the Xhosa People. London: Jonathan Cape.

Steinberg, Jonny. (2004). *Nongoloza's Children: Western Cape prison gangs during and after apartheid.* Monograph written for the Centre for the Study of Violence and Reconciliation, July 2004.

Steinberg, Jonny. (2004). *The Number: One Man's Search for Identity in the Cape Underworld and Prison Gangs.* Cape Town: Jonathan Ball Publishers.

Van Onselen, Charles. (1982). *New Babylon and New Nineveh: Everyday Life on the Witwatersrand 1886–1914.* Cape Town: Jonathan Ball Publishers.

Van Onselen, Charles. (1985). *The Small Matter of a Horse: The Life of 'Nongoloza' Mathebula 1867–1948.* Johannesburg: Ravan Press.

Vearey, Jeremy. (n.d.). *Nongoloza's Legacy: Prison and Street Gangs in the Western Cape* (SAPS report).

WHEN THE EARTH SHOOK

Penn, Nigel. (2015). *Murderers, Miscreants and Mutineers: Early Colonial Cape Lives.* Johannesburg: Jacana.

Green, Lawrence George. (1951). *Grow Lovely, Growing Old: Cape Town.* Cape Town: Howard Timmins.

Strassberger, Elfriede. (1969). *The Rhenish Mission Society in South Africa 1830–1950.* Cape Town: C. Struik.

Theron, Jan. (2016). *Solidarity Road: The Story of a Trade Union in the Ending of Apartheid.* Johannesburg: Jacana.

'THE BATONS SLIP OUT OF YOUR HANDS WHEN THEY ARE COVERED IN BLOOD'

Centre for Conflict Resolution. (2003). The Voorberg Story: The Centre for Conflict Resolution Prisons Transformation Programme in Voorberg Prison.

Giddy, Patrick. (2018). The human spirit and its appropriation: Ethics, psyche and religious symbology in the context of evolution. *Religion and Theology* 25: 88–110.

Giffard, Chris. (2002). Restorative Justice in Prisons: An option for South Africa? *Track Two* 11(2): 34–38.

International Centre for Prison Studies. (2002). *'We don't waste prisoners' time and we don't waste bicycles': The impact of restorative work in prisons.* London: International Centre for Prison Studies.

News24. (2016). Prison gang violence leaves Brandvlei warders traumatised – expert. 21 November 2016. Available at https://www.news24.com/News24/prison-gang-violence-leaves-brandvlei-warders-traumatised-expert-20161121 (accessed 13 December 2021).

Pogrund, Benjamin. (2000). *War of Words: Memoir of a South African Journalist.* New York, NY: Seven Stories Press, pp. 160–187.

Restorative Justice Council. (n.d.). Principles of Restorative Practice. Available at https://restorativejustice.org.uk (accessed 13 December 2021).

Van Zyl Smit, Dirk. (1992). *South African Prison Law and Practice.* Durban: Butterworths.

Venter, HJ. (1959). *Die Geskiedenis van die Suid*

Afrikaanse Gevangenisstelsel 1652–1958. Pretoria: University of Pretoria.

Zehr, Howard. (2002). *The Little Book of Restorative Justice*. Intercourse, PA: Good Books.

PREPARATION

Gould, Chandré. (2012). *Beaten bad: The life stories of violent offenders*. Monograph: Institute for Security Studies. Available at https://issafrica.org/research/monographs/beaten-bad-the-life-stories-of-violent-offenders (accessed 13 December 2021).

Hoffman, Sandy. (2012). *Disrespected*. Self-published.